UNDERSTANDING
Illuminated Manuscripts

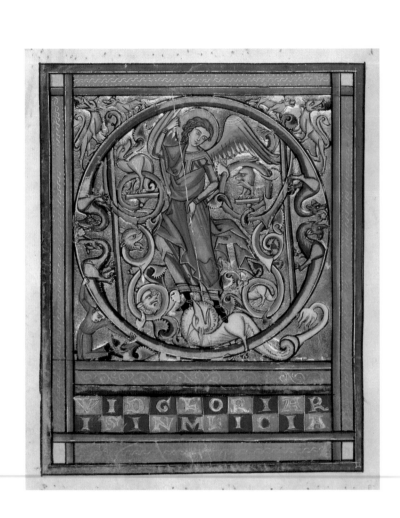

UNDERSTANDING
ILLUMINATED MANUSCRIPTS

A GUIDE TO TECHNICAL TERMS

Michelle P. Brown

THE J. PAUL GETTY MUSEUM
in association with
THE BRITISH LIBRARY

© 1994 The J. Paul Getty Museum and
The British Library Board

Second printing, 1995

Published by
The J. Paul Getty Museum
17985 Pacific Coast Highway
Malibu, California 90265-5799
in association with
The British Library

At the J. Paul Getty Museum:
Christopher Hudson, Publisher
John Harris, Editor

At the J. Paul Getty Trust Publication Services:
Richard R. Kinney, Director
Deenie Yudell, Design Manager
Karen Schmidt, Production Manager

Library of Congress Cataloging-in-Publication Data

Brown, Michelle.
    Understanding illuminated manuscripts : a guide to technical
terms / Michelle P. Brown.
        p.   cm.
    Includes bibliographical references.
    ISBN 0-89236-217-0
    1. Illumination of books and manuscripts—Dictionaries.
I. Title.
ND2889.B76   1994
745.6'7'0940902—dc20   93-42239
                                                          CIP

Cover: *A Boat Docked to a Whale*. Bestiary and other texts. France, c.
1270. 19×14.4 cm (7½×5¹¹⁄₁₆ in.). JPGM, Ms. Ludwig XV 3
(83.MR.173), fol. 89v (detail).

Frontispiece: Initial *Q* with *Saint Michael Battling the Dragon*. Psalter.
Germany (Würzburg), c. 1240–50. 22.6×15.7 cm (8⅞×6³⁄₁₆ in.).
JPGM, Ms. Ludwig VIII 2 (83.MK.93), fol. 61v.

This guide is designed to provide information for the public, students, and professionals alike about the history of manuscript production and its study: the contexts of production and the people involved (contained in entries such as SCRIBE, ILLUMINATOR, MASTER, WORKSHOP, STATIONER, PATRON, SCRIPTORIUM, MONASTIC PRODUCTION, and SECULAR PRODUCTION); the physical processes and techniques employed (CODICOLOGY); the types of text encountered (from liturgical volumes used in the performance of the MASS and DIVINE OFFICE and others, such as the BOOK OF HOURS, made for private devotions, to CLASSICAL and MEDICAL TEXTS as well as the ROMANCES and APOCALYPSES commissioned by secular patrons); and the terminology applied to the elements, styles, and forms of ILLUMINATION.

Understanding Illuminated Manuscripts covers works made in the West from Antiquity until the early modern period and the establishment of printing, but reference is also made to later periods when relevant. The manuscript production of non-Western cultures could not be included, since such subjects as Hebrew and Islamic manuscripts are complex fields in their own right. However, important influences of non-Western cultures on the production of manuscripts in the West are cited in various entries.

I should like to thank the following for their invaluable advice and assistance on this project: the staff of the manuscripts department and the photographic, publication, and design offices of the J. Paul Getty Museum and the British Library, especially Thomas Kren, Janet Backhouse, John Harris, Kurt Hauser, Elizabeth Teviotdale, Jane Carr, David Way, Peter Kidd, Erik Inglis, and Nancy Turner; as well as Linda Brownrigg, Philip Lewis, Sheila Schwartz, and Patricia Stirnemann. I should also like to acknowledge a particular debt of gratitude to William Noel for his unstinting assistance and friendship and to my husband, Cecil Brown, for his understanding and support during this endeavor, as ever.

M. P. B.

HEAD

Raised
split cord

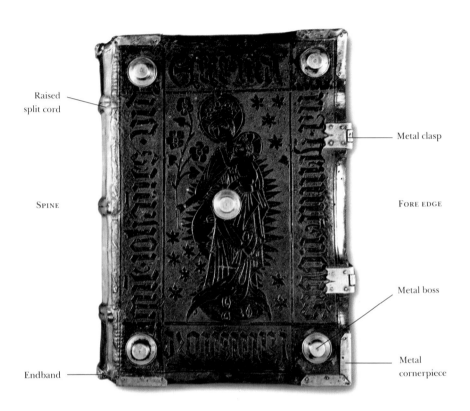

Metal clasp

SPINE

FORE EDGE

Metal boss

Endband

Metal
cornerpiece

Blind stamped
and tooled tanned
leather cover
depicting the
Virgin and Child

TAIL

Front cover. Peter Comestor, *Historia scholastica*. Germany (Amorbach?), 1451.
28.8 × 21.5 cm (11 5/16 × 8 7/16 in.). BL, Add. Ms. 18972.

Head

Strap (and pin)

Spine

Split cord

Ex libris inscription of Fountains Abbey, co. York, 1658

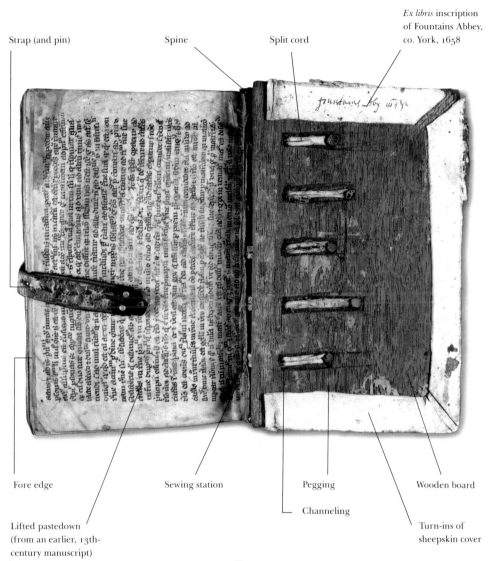

Fore edge

Sewing station

Pegging

Wooden board

Channeling

Lifted pastedown (from an earlier, 13th-century manuscript)

Turn-ins of sheepskin cover

Tail

Inside back cover. *Parabole Salomonis* and other texts. England (Fountains Abbey), late 13th or early 14th century. Leaf: 19.3 × 13.2 cm (7⅝ × 5³⁄₁₆ in.). BL, Add. Ms. 62130.

Miniature depicting
the Visitation

Gilded frame

Foliate border,
incorporating
strawberries and a
pot of carnations

Unfinished
heraldic device

Rubric
(in red)

Decorated initial
D, composed of
branches on a
foliate ground

Script

Line fillers
(one in the form of
a branch, the other
a decorated bar)

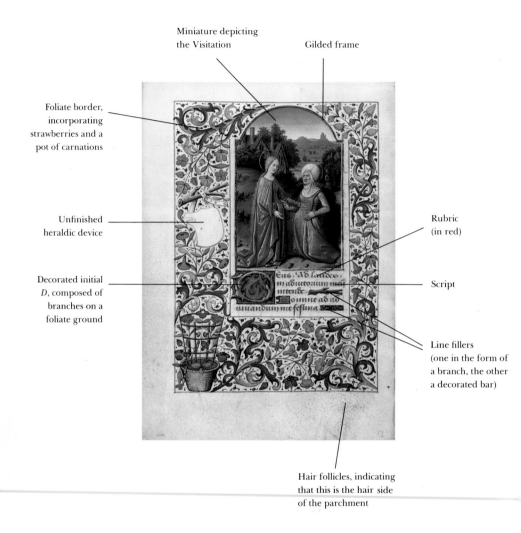

Hair follicles, indicating
that this is the hair side
of the parchment

Jean Bourdichon. *The Visitation.* Book of hours. France, c. 1480–85.
16.3 × 11.6 cm (6⁷/₁₆ × 4⁹/₁₆ in.). JPGM, Ms. 6 (84.ML.746), fol. 41v.

ABBREVIATION

Abbreviations were often used to save space and effort when writing. They generally fall into three categories: *suspensions*, in which the end of a word is abbreviated, signaled by the use of a horizontal bar or another graphic symbol; *contractions*, in which another part of a word is abbreviated with the use of a graphic symbol; *abbreviation symbols*, used for whole words and often derived from the tachygraphic (shorthand) systems of ANTIQUITY (that of Tiro, Cicero's secretary, being most influential). All three types of abbreviation could be used in the same manuscript, as variable and invariable forms and as phonetic equivalents.

During Antiquity a few common elements were often abbreviated (notably the Latin word endings *-bus* and *-que* and the final *m* and *n*). These short forms are known as *notae communes*, while abbreviations for specialized jargon in legal texts are known as *notae iuris*. Abbreviations for *nomina sacra* ("sacred names"), such as the Greek *xp̄s* form of *Christus* (see CHI-RHO), occur in EARLY CHRISTIAN works. INSULAR scribes were especially fond of abbreviations, including tironian *notae*, and Irish scribes used them extensively in order to produce pocket-size GOSPEL BOOKS for study purposes (pocket Gospels). With the growth of universities, from around 1200, the use of abbreviations proliferated. Medieval readers would have been familiar with such devices, although there were probably always some that were particularly obscure, and there is evidence that SCRIBES themselves sometimes puzzled over certain abbreviations.

ACANTHUS

A foliate motif much used in medieval art and derived from the depiction of the acanthus plant in a decorative context during ANTIQUITY. Medieval renditions of the acanthus are generally not as true to the actual plant as those of Antiquity, reducing it to a cipher consisting of STYLIZED fleshy fronds. Acanthus ornament was particularly favored by the CAROLINGIANS, for whom it represented a conscious revival of a Mediterranean form. See the illustration accompanying BENEDICTIONAL.

Note Words printed in SMALL CAPITALS refer to other entries in the book.

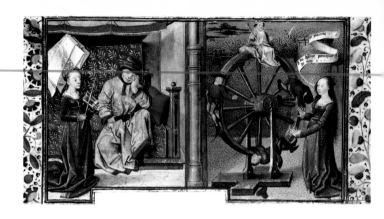

ALLEGORY

A symbolic depiction of an idea. For example, the vagaries of fortune were often symbolized visually by a female figure, Fortuna, turning a wheel upon which figures from varied walks of life rise and fall.

ALUM TAWED

Alum tawing is a process for preparing white leather by soaking animal skin in alum (potassium aluminum sulfate).

ANGLO-SAXON

The Anglo-Saxon period extended from c. 500 to 1066. During this time, England was largely occupied and ruled by GERMANIC peoples, primarily the Angles and the Saxons. Prior to the Viking incursions of the ninth century, the culture of England interacted closely with that of CELTIC Britain and Ireland. The art produced during the four centuries from c. 550 to 900 is often termed INSULAR, reflecting this interaction among the peoples inhabiting the regions that we know as the British Isles and Ireland. With reference to ILLUMINATION, the term Anglo-Saxon is often reserved for the period after 900.

During the tenth century, two major Anglo-Saxon painting styles developed, largely under the influence of Insular and CAROLINGIAN models. The first, or *Winchester*, style is so named because certain of its key examples, such as the BENEDICTIONAL of Saint Ethelwold, were probably made at Winchester, even though the style was diffused throughout the region. It is characterized by an opulent manner of painting, with rich colors and GILDING (unless executed in a TINTED or OUTLINE DRAWING style), a NATURALISTIC figure style, fluttering, decorative drapery, and a heavy ACANTHUS-like ornament. This style exhibits the influence of Carolingian art, specifically the Court School of Charlemagne, the School of Metz, and the Franco-Saxon School (which employed INTERLACE motifs ultimately of Insular inspiration), and is also indebted to BYZANTINE art. The second major style, the *Utrecht* style, was inspired by the Utrecht PSALTER, an important Carolingian manuscript that featured an agitated, sketchy, and ILLUSIONISTIC form of outline drawing adopted from classical painting technique. During the first half of the eleventh century, the Winchester and Utrecht styles began to fuse. Scandinavian art also exerted a limited influence during the Anglo-Saxon period.

Anglo-Saxon art continued to exchange influences with art on the Continent and made a significant contribution to the formation of ROMANESQUE art. It also developed a number of sophisticated ICONOGRAPHIES, based on interpretative, exegetical literature (important themes include the Trinity, the Crucifixion, the Virgin, the evangelists, and David). See the illustrations accompanying BENEDICTIONAL, LIBER VITAE, OUTLINE DRAWING, and TROPER.

ANTHROPOMORPHIC INITIAL

An INITIAL composed wholly or partly of human figures. Anthropomorphic motifs occur in other decorative contexts as well.

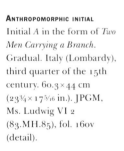

ANTHROPOMORPHIC INITIAL
Initial *A* in the form of *Two Men Carrying a Branch*. Gradual. Italy (Lombardy), third quarter of the 15th century. 60.3×44 cm (23¾ × 17⁵⁄₁₆ in.). JPGM, Ms. Ludwig VI 2 (83.MH.85), fol. 160v (detail).

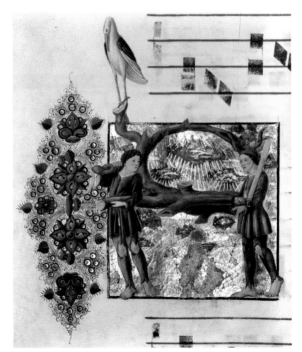

ANTIPHONAL

An antiphonal, also called antiphoner or antiphonary, contains the sung portions of the DIVINE OFFICE. Such books are often large in format, so that they could be used by a choir, and include DECORATED and HISTORIATED INITIALS, depicting saints and key events of the liturgical year. Hymns are usually contained in a separate volume.

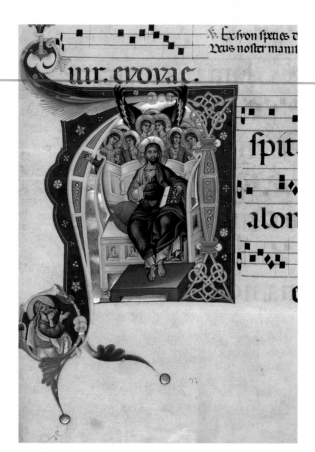

Originally, the antiphonal may have included chants sung in
the MASS, but its use became restricted to the Divine Office during
the CAROLINGIAN period, and the GRADUAL became the principal
CHOIR BOOK for the mass. The contents of the antiphonal are
generally arranged in accordance with the TEMPORALE, SANCTO-
RALE, and Common of Saints in liturgical order.

ANTIQUITY

The classical world of Greece and Rome, prior to the decline of
the Roman Empire during the fifth century and the occupation
of much of its former territory by barbarian peoples. Certain of
these peoples, notably the Ostrogoths and the Visigoths, were
more inclined than others to promote continuity with the culture
of the conquered regions. As a result, the transition from late
Antiquity to the early Middle Ages was relatively gradual in some
areas—for example, Italy, Spain, and parts of Gaul. The BYZAN-
TINE Empire, which withstood the barbarian onslaught, became
the cultural and political heir of much of what had been the eastern part of the Roman Empire.

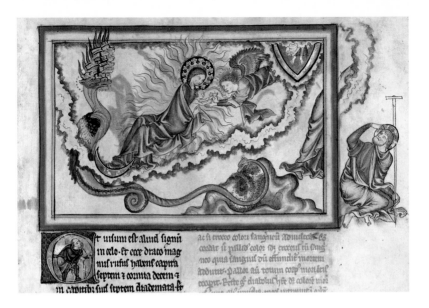

APOCALYPSE

The biblical book known in the Protestant tradition as the Book
of Revelation. During the Middle Ages, Apocalypse manuscripts
were produced in Latin and Anglo-Norman versions often accompanied by COMMENTARIES, such as that of Berengaudus, and
sometimes with PICTURE CYCLES of varying length, style, and technique. These cycles catered to a wide range of PATRONS.

Although known during the early Middle Ages, Apocalypse
manuscripts were particularly popular in tenth- and eleventh-
century Spain, where the scriptural text was integrated with the
commentary of Beatus of Liébana (c. 776) and produced in lavishly illustrated copies in Mozarabic style. They were also popular
in England for a brief time (c. 1250–75), with production probably centered in London. Apocalypse manuscripts proliferated
during the thirteenth century, possibly due to escalating fears concerning the Antichrist (associated by many with the Holy Roman
Emperor, Frederick II, 1194–1250), the approach of the Tartar
hordes, and the coming of the Last Judgment. Use of the text as
an ALLEGORY of personal Christian experience may also have
added to its appeal. See the illustration accompanying GILDING.

APPLIED COVERS

Decorative plaques, generally of metalwork or ivory, which are set
into or onto the BOARDS of a BINDING. They are encountered from
the EARLY CHRISTIAN period on.

Arabesque	An ornament or style of ornamentation consisting of fine, linear foliate designs in curvilinear patterns, derived from Islamic art.

Arabic numerals	The figures 0–9, introduced into Europe from India, via the Islamic world, around 1100. From the thirteenth century on, the use of Arabic numerals increased, partially supplanting ROMAN NUMERALS and other alphabetic systems of numeric representation. They did not come into general use, however, until the fifteenth century.

Astronomical/ astrological texts	Manuscripts on the subject of astronomy or astrology often contain images associated with the constellations (such as Orion the hunter and Aquarius the water bearer) or diagrammatic representations of the universe and its components. Some of the major astronomical texts to appear in illuminated copies include: Cicero's *Aratea*, written in the first century B.C., a Latin translation of a third-century B.C. Greek verse text by Aratus, in turn based on a prose treatise, the *Phoenomena*, written by Eudoxus of Cnidos a century earlier; Ptolemy's *Almagest* (c. 142 A.D.); and later medieval compositions, such as John Foxton's *Liber Cosmographiae*. See also MEDICAL TEXTS and COMPUTUS TEXTS.

Astronomy (the observation of the stars, or "natural astrology") was not originally distinguished from astrology (divination by means of the observation of the stars, or "judicial astrology"). In the fourth century B.C., for example, Aristotle used "astrology" to embrace both subjects. The Mesopotamians and Egyptians were instrumental in the early development of astronomy and astrology and identified each of the heavenly bodies with specific gods. Their practices were transmitted to the Greek and Roman worlds and subsequently to Islam and the medieval West. The study of

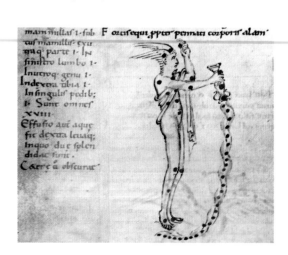

ASTRONOMICAL/ASTROLOGICAL
TEXTS
The Constellation Aquarius.
Cicero, *Aratea* and other
astronomical treatises.
France (Fleury), late 10th
century. 29.3 × 21.2 cm
(11⁹⁄₁₆ × 8⅜ in.). BL, Harley
Ms. 2506, fol. 38v (detail).

both astronomy and astrology declined in the first Christian centuries, the latter because its system of prognostication ran counter to the preordained plan of Christian salvation. In the CAROLINGIAN period, however, with its revival of CLASSICAL TEXTS, both subjects were taken up again. As a result, certain works, such as CALENDARS and horoscopes, were used in conjunction with both astronomical and astrological material.

From the twelfth century, Arabic learning, which had preserved aspects of classical knowledge in astronomy and astrology as well as other subjects, increasingly influenced the West. Western thinkers became interested in the works of Eudoxus, Ptolemy, and Al-Bitruji (fl. c. 1190), and by the thirteenth century a controversy even arose (in which the theologian Albertus Magnus and the philosopher-scientist Roger Bacon played an important part) concerning the respective merits of the ancient and Arabic authors. The rise of new methods of astronomy during the fifteenth century and the 1543 publication of Nicolaus Copernicus' theory that the earth revolved around the sun did much to damage the academic credibility of astrology, but it continued to exert an influence within society. Moreover, there was never a clear-cut division between works in these fields and those dealing with experimental science, alchemy, and magic.

ATELIER

See WORKSHOP.

ATTRIBUTE

An object that identifies a person, most often used for saints. Saint Catherine, for example, is usually depicted with the wheel, the instrument of her martyrdom.

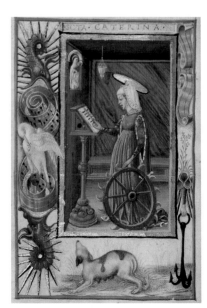

ATTRIBUTE
Taddeo Crivelli. *Saint Catherine with Her Wheel.* Gualenghi-d'Este Hours. Italy (Ferrara), c. 1470. 10.8 × 7.9 cm (4¼ × 3⅛ in.). JPGM, Ms. Ludwig IX 13 (83.ML.109), fol. 187v.

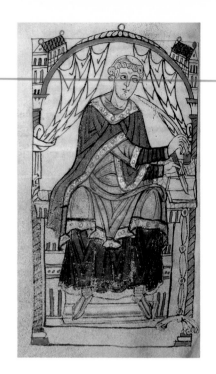

AUTHOR PORTRAIT A MINIATURE or HISTORIATED INITIAL depicting the author of a text. Author portraits were known in ANTIQUITY and appear in manuscripts throughout the Middle Ages in a variety of texts.

BANDS See CORDS.

BAS-DE-PAGE Bas-de-page (literally, "bottom of the page") scenes are usually unframed images that may or may not refer to the text or image above. They are found in GOTHIC illumination from the thirteenth century on.

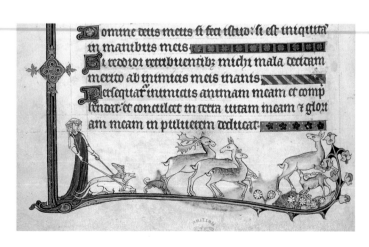

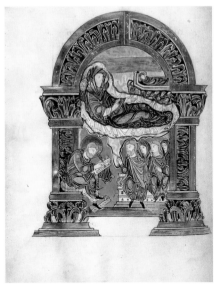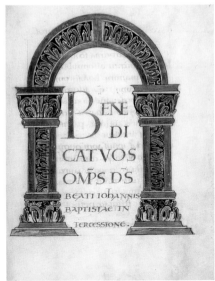

BENEDICTIONAL

The Nativity and Naming of John the Baptist; decorated incipit page. Benedictional of Saint Ethelwold.
England (Winchester?), 971–84. Leaf: 29.5 × 22 cm (11⅝ × 8¹¹⁄₁₆ in.). BL, Add. Ms. 49598, fols. 92v–93.

BENEDICTIONAL

A SERVICE BOOK consisting of a collection of episcopal blessings, delivered during the MASS after the *Pater noster* and arranged according to the liturgical year. Some lavishly illuminated examples were produced in ANGLO-SAXON England for individual bishops such as Saint Ethelwold of Winchester.

BESTIARY

The *Bestiarius, De Bestiis,* or *Book of Beasts* consists of descriptions and tales of animals, birds, fantastic creatures, and stones, real and imaginary, which are imbued with Christian symbolism or moral lessons. The rising of the phoenix from the pyre, for example, is related to Christ's Resurrection.

The bestiary, in all its varied manifestations, enjoyed great popularity during the twelfth and thirteenth centuries, especially in England. Among the most beloved of picture books, a favorite of the literate laity, it functioned as a LIBRARY and SCHOOL BOOK and as homiletic source material. The text was frequently illustrated, in styles catering to a variety of purses, and motifs drawn from it are widely encountered in other decorative contexts, including BAS-DE-PAGE scenes, HERALDRY, and encyclopedic world maps (see MAPPA MUNDI).

The core of the text originated in the writings of authors such

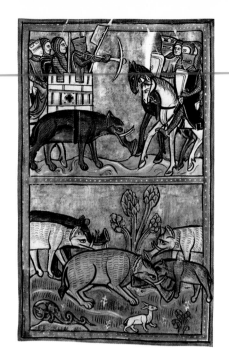

as Herodotus, Aristotle, and Pliny the Elder, and in a Greek text known as the *Physiologus* (*The Natural Philosopher*), which is thought to have been compiled in Alexandria around the second century by a Christian ascetic. In the *Physiologus*, discussions of the characteristics of almost fifty creatures, plants, and stones, along with the etymologies of their names, were distilled from classical mythology and the Christian tradition.

The *Physiologus* was influential for a thousand years, being translated into Arabic, Armenian, Ethiopic, Syriac, and other VERNACULAR languages; the later medieval bestiaries descended primarily from a variable Latin translation that was available from at least the fifth century. Several more beasts and additional material were conflated with the Latin *Physiologus* from the *Etymologies* of the seventh-century Spanish bishop Isidore of Seville and other selected sources. From this expanded text, Philippe de Thaon produced a rhyming version in Anglo-Norman (c. 1125), dedicated to Aelis de Louvain, second wife of Henry I of England; this version gave rise to the popular medieval *Bestiaire*. Other medieval versions include that of Gervaise, written in French (perhaps in Normandy) in the thirteenth century; that of Guillaume le Clerc (the most popular version), written in the early thirteenth century in French by a Norman priest working in England; and two versions ascribed to Pierre de Beauvais, "le Picard," composed in the dialect of Picardy, also in the early thirteenth century. The Latin bestiary still flourished alongside its French counterparts and was often produced in luxurious illustrated copies in England during the twelfth and thirteenth centuries. These are grouped into two important families on the basis of variations in their texts and programs of ILLUMINATION.

BIANCHI GIRARI   See WHITE VINE-STEM.

BIBLE   A number of Latin versions of books of the Bible, translated from Greek and Hebrew, were used in the EARLY CHRISTIAN Church; these are known as *Old Latin* versions. To establish a measure of uniformity among these various translations, Saint Jerome, encouraged by Pope Damasus I, undertook a new translation of the whole Bible, working from the Greek and the Hebrew for the Old Testament. The translation he produced, begun about 382 and completed in 404, is known as the *Vulgate*. The work went through several stages, including three versions of the Psalms (Roman, Gallican, and Hebrew). Throughout the Middle Ages it was common for books of the Bible to be contained in separate volumes (such as the PENTATEUCH, HEXATEUCH, OCTATEUCH, or the Gospels). For liturgical purposes, scriptural texts (or readings from them) were often incorporated into SERVICE BOOKS (such as EVANGELARIES, EPISTOLARIES, and PSALTERS).

BIBLE
Text page including initial
I with *Christ and the Prophet
Zacharias*. Glossed Bible.
France (Paris?), 13th
century. 49.5 × 32 cm
(19½ × 12⅝ in.). BL, Add.
Ms. 15253, fol. 247v.

Beginning in the fourth century, when Christianity gradually became the official religion of the Roman Empire, luxurious CODICES were produced, among them the Codex Sinaiticus and the Cotton Genesis. During the early Middle Ages, corruptions of the Vulgate and intrusions from Old Latin versions led several scholars to attempt to standardize the biblical texts; Cassiodorus in the sixth century and, in the CAROLINGIAN period, Alcuin of York, Theodulf of Orléans, and Hartmut of St. Gall are the best known of these. As a result of their endeavors, a group of large, luxuriously written and illuminated editions of the complete Bible were produced. Cassiodorus' nine-volume edition influenced Bible manuscripts in ANGLO-SAXON England, such as the Codex Amiatinus, and in the ninth century Alcuin's SCRIPTORIUM at Tours went on to produce a whole series of Bibles for circulation. During the ROMANESQUE period, many of the Bibles produced were large in format. In the late twelfth and thirteenth centuries, a practice arose, stimulated by the universities, of producing small-format Bibles (or parts thereof) with condensed SCRIPT and HISTORIATED INITIALS, often accompanied by GLOSSES. Many of these were made quite cheaply.

Scriptural texts were translated into the VERNACULAR as early as the eighth century (in Anglo-Saxon England), generally as glosses, but many of the major developments in vernacular translation took place from the fourteenth to the sixteenth century, beginning with John Wycliffe, who made the first complete translation of the Bible into English; the German translation made by Martin Luther in the 1520s is still in use today.

BIBLE HISTORIALE

The biblical narrative in prose form, written by Guyart des Moulins and based on his translation into French (1291–94) of the *Historia scholastica* of Peter Comestor, interspersed with a French translation of the BIBLE produced in Paris around 1250. The illustrations accompanying the *Bible historiale* (usually in the form of COLUMN PICTURES) depict many scenes not normally found in the standard repertory of biblical images and also include representations of the compilation and translation of the text.

BIBLE MORALISÉE

The most important type of medieval picture BIBLE, also known as the *Bible historiée*, *Bible allégorisée*, or *Emblèmes bibliques*. Composed during the thirteenth century, it consists of short biblical passages and related COMMENTARIES with moral or allegorical lessons. These latter usually emphasized the connections between Old and New Testament events (see TYPOLOGY). The texts were accompanied by extensive illustrations. The most sumptuous extant *Bible moralisée* contains about five thousand images, in medallion form, and is arranged in columns. Other sorts of picture Bibles also existed (see BIBLIA PAUPERUM).

BIBLIA PAUPERUM

Literally, the "BIBLE of the Poor," it consisted of a series of captioned MINIATURES illustrating the parallels between the Old and New Testaments (see TYPOLOGY). Scenes from the life of Christ are accompanied by Old Testament scenes and figures of the prophets. Although few have survived, such books are known to have been very popular during the later Middle Ages, especially as a tool for religious instruction among poorer clergy and those members of LAY society who, although often quite wealthy, were not especially learned. The BIBLE MORALISÉE is another type of picture book based on the Bible.

BIFOLIUM
(pl. BIFOLIA)

A sheet of writing support material (generally PARCHMENT during the Middle Ages) folded in half to produce two leaves (i.e., four pages). A number of bifolia folded together form a QUIRE.

BINDER

A person wholly or partly responsible for sewing a CODEX together and supplying it with covers. Although there is evidence that SCRIBES occasionally undertook the preliminary "tacket" sewing of their own sections of manuscripts, the binder was often another member of the SCRIPTORIUM. Following the rise of universities in the late twelfth century, BINDING became the preserve of the STATIONER. The term binder can also be used of a BINDING MEDIUM.

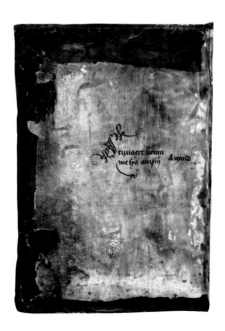

BINDER
Binder's colophon. Book of hours. Bound in Ghent or Bruges, c. 1450–60. 19.4 × 14 cm (7⅝ × 5½ in.). JPGM, Ms. 2 (84.ML.67), pastedown.

The colophon records that the book was bound by Lievin Stuvaert of Ghent.

BINDING

The sewing and covering of a book. When the leaves of a CODEX had been written and illuminated, they were assembled into gatherings (QUIRES) and sewn together. Generally they were sewn onto supports (CORDS), although there also existed an unsupported form of sewing in which only the thread served to bind the quires together (COPTIC SEWING). The loose ends of the cords were then attached to BOARDS, normally of wood (see CHANNELING and PEGGING), which were then covered, usually with damp leather. The covering could be decorated in a number of ways (see APPLIED COVERS, BLOCKED, CHEMISE BINDING, CUT LEATHER, PANELS, TANNED, and TOOLED). CLASPS or STRAP AND PIN mechanisms would then be attached to hold the book in shape, and BOSSES might be added to protect the binding. Binding was generally undertaken in the SCRIPTORIUM or by STATIONERS. See also BINDER, CHAINED BOOK, ENDBANDS, GAUFFERED, KETTLE STITCH, LIMP BINDING, PASTEDOWN, SEWING ON SUPPORTS, SEWING STATIONS, STAPLE, and TITLE PIECE.

BINDING MEDIUM

An ingredient in paint or INK that binds the PIGMENT and makes it adhere to the surface to be embellished. Clarified egg white (glair, *clarea*) was the principal binding medium used in manuscript ILLUMINATION. Gum (such as gum arabic from the acacia), glue (such as ichthyocollon, a fish glue, and casein, a dairy-product glue) or other forms of size (PARCHMENT size or gelatin) were also used for this purpose as well as for GILDING.

BLIND TOOLED

See TOOLED.

BLOCKED

A technique of decorating BINDINGS in which a design or picture is stamped into the leather cover by a block, into which the image has been carved or incised. Large woodblocks were sometimes employed for this purpose in the Netherlands during the sixteenth century. Metal blocks were first used in Flanders, allegedly by a canon of Antwerp, Wouter van Duffle, in the early thirteenth century. See also PANELS and TOOLED.

BOARDS

The stiff covers at the front and back of a book. Wood was the material generally used until the early sixteenth century, preferably oak or another hardwood to minimize worming. These covers could be very thick and often had beveled edges. Pasteboard became popular in the sixteenth century; from the late seventeenth century on, it was supplemented by rope-fiber millboards. Strawboard first came into use in the eighteenth century. The boards were attached to the QUIRES by the CORDS, which were

threaded through the boards and secured (often by means of PEG-
GING). The boards and SPINE were then usually covered with
damp leather (although PARCHMENT, fabric, or PAPER might also
be used), which was folded over the edges of the boards (forming
what are known as TURN-INS) and glued down. PASTEDOWNS could
then be applied to conceal this mechanism.

BOOKMARKER

A variety of devices for marking key openings in a book have survived, most of them dating from the twelfth century on. Tabs or
knotted strips of PARCHMENT, sometimes colored, were attached to
the FORE EDGE of the book at appropriate points; ribbons of linen,
silk, or parchment could be attached to the headband (see END-
BANDS) and descend vertically into the book. Some bookmarkers
even carry a device used in conjunction with the text to be marked,
such as a VOLVELLE to assist in relevant chronological or astronomical calculations. Flowers and other pressed organic materials
were also used as bookmarkers.

BOOK OF HOURS

A book, also called a *primer* or *horae*, for use in private devotions.
Its central text, the Little Office of the Blessed Virgin (or Hours
of the Virgin), is modeled on the DIVINE OFFICE and represents a
shorter version of the devotions performed at the eight canonical
hours. The text, known from the tenth century, was originally
read only by ecclesiastics; it entered into more popular use by the
end of the twelfth century, often being attached to the PSALTER,

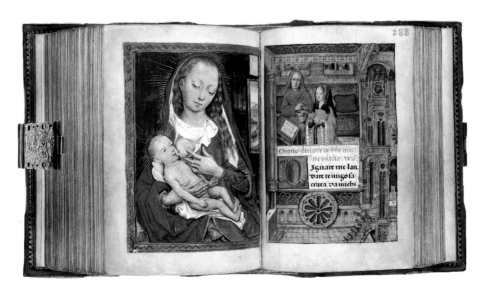

BOOK OF HOURS

Joanna the Mad in Prayer before the Virgin and Child. Hours of Joanna of Castile. Belgium (Ghent or Bruges),
1496–1506. Leaf: 11 × 7.5 cm (4⁵⁄₁₆ × 2¹⁵⁄₁₆ in.). BL, Add. Ms. 18852, fols. 287v–288.

the book more commonly used for private devotions before the emergence of the book of hours. The private recitation of the Little Office of the Virgin is an expression of the LAY person's desire to imitate the prayer-life of the religious.

The Little Office of the Virgin gradually acquired other elements: a liturgical CALENDAR, a LITANY OF THE SAINTS, SUFFRAGES, the Office of the Dead (which had emerged by the ninth century), the Penitential Psalms (Psalms 6, 31, 37, 50, 101, 129, and 142, which were first included in books of hours in the thirteenth century), the Gradual Psalms (Psalms 119–133), and prayers. Additional offices, such as the Short Office of the Cross, Hours of the Holy Spirit, Hours of the Trinity, and Hours of the Passion, could also form part of a book of hours. The book of hours took its standard form in the thirteenth century and continued in general use until the sixteenth century, enjoying particular popularity in France and Flanders. The texts of books of hours vary slightly in accordance with USE.

Books of hours were medieval best-sellers and have survived in relatively high quantity. They are nearly always illuminated, in a manner commensurate with the PATRON's budget, and often contain a MINIATURE or set of miniatures for each major textual division. These subjects include scenes from the life of the Virgin, Christ, and King David, depictions of the saints and themes relating to death and judgment. The patron was also sometimes portrayed. Decorated letters as well as images can be found in books of hours. See also the illustrations accompanying ATTRIBUTE, CALENDAR, ILLUSIONISTIC, LITANY OF THE SAINTS, MASTER, PATRON, and RINCEAUX.

BOOKPLATE

See EX LIBRIS INSCRIPTION.

BORDER

Decorative surrounds, or borders, were popular in GOTHIC and RENAISSANCE illumination and evolved during the thirteenth century from the extenders that sprang from decorated letters. A border surrounds text and/or image and may occupy margins and intercolumnar space. Some borders are in paneled form, others are composed of foliate decoration or bars, the latter often sprouting plant forms and known as *foliate bar borders*. A full border surrounds an image or text on all sides, while a partial border frames only part of the area in question. Like an INITIAL, a border can be INHABITED or HISTORIATED. During the fifteenth century, a form of border became popular (initially within the works of the Ghent-Bruges School and subsequently in French and Italian illumination) in which naturalistically rendered flora and fauna were placed, as if strewn, on a ground (often gilded). These are termed *scatter, strewn,* or TROMPE L'OEIL borders. Another popular form of border during the fourteenth and fifteenth centuries was the

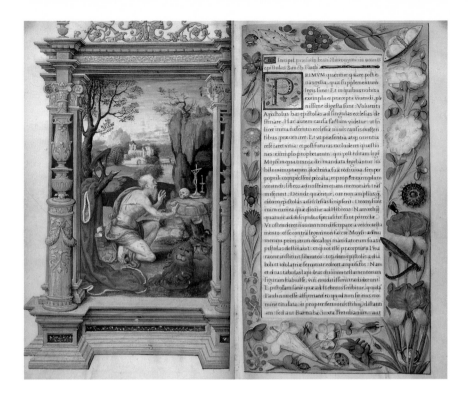

spray border, consisting of fine foliate tendrils with small gilded leaves. HUMANISTIC manuscripts often feature WHITE VINE-STEM borders. See the illustrations accompanying MASTER and RINCEAUX.

BOSS

A protruding ornament, usually of metal. When applied to a binding it serves a protective function. Metalwork plaques are known to have adorned bindings from the EARLY CHRISTIAN period on, but prominent raised bosses appear to have become popular during the fifteenth century.

BOUNDING LINES

The marginal lines supplied during RULING to guide the justification of the text and its ancillaries (such as INITIALS).

BREVIARY

A SERVICE BOOK containing the texts necessary for the celebration of the DIVINE OFFICE. A breviary is often adorned with DECORATED or HISTORIATED INITIALS, and more luxurious copies may

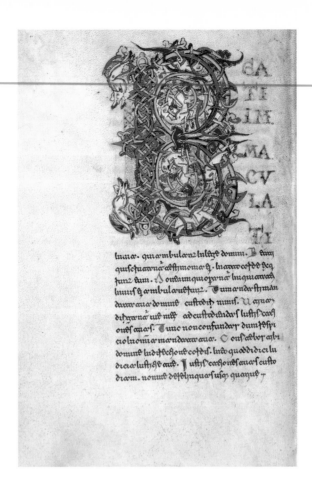

BREVIARY
Inhabited initial *B*.
Breviary. Italy (Monte
Cassino), 1153. 19.1 × 13.2
cm (7 ½ × 5 3/16 in.). JPGM,
Ms. Ludwig IX 1
(83.ML.97), fol. 216v.

contain MINIATURES depicting biblical scenes or the performance
of the office.

From the eleventh century on, the various volumes used during the Divine Office (PSALTER, ANTIPHONAL, LECTIONARY, COL-
LECTAR, MARTYROLOGY, and others) were combined to form the
breviary, which was initially only used by monks, but was popularized (in slightly abridged form) by the Dominicans and Francis-
cans in the thirteenth century. The breviary's contents were
divided into TEMPORALE, SANCTORALE, and Common of Saints.
All members of monastic orders and the clergy in major orders
are committed to the daily recitation of the breviary. The contents
vary in detail in accordance with the rite of the religious order or
the USE of the geographic area.

BRUSH

Brushes of animal hair set within wooden handles were used in
medieval ILLUMINATION, replacing the frayed reed brushes of
ANTIQUITY. The quill PEN could be used to apply certain paints as
well as INKS.

BURGUNDIAN

Loyset Liédet. *Lydia's Sons Sentenced to Death.* David Aubert, *Histoire de Charles Martel.* Belgium (written in Brussels and illuminated in Bruges), c. 1463–72. 23.5 × 19.5 cm (9¼ × 7¹¹⁄₁₆ in.). JPGM, Ms. Ludwig XIII 6 (83.MP.149), leaf 12.

This manuscript was commissioned by Duke Philip the Good of Burgundy (1419–67), and later was illuminated for his successor, Duke Charles the Bold (1467–77).

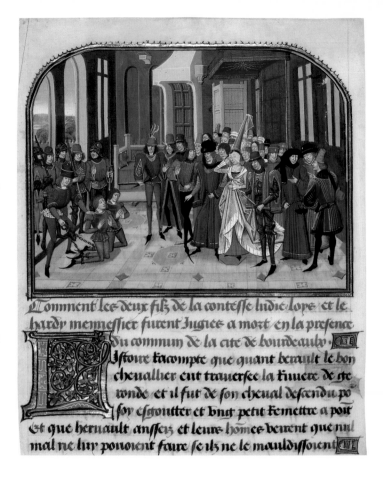

BURGUNDIAN

Used of a courtly style of art that flourished under the patronage of the Dukes of Burgundy, primarily in Flanders, from the late fourteenth to the mid-sixteenth century.

Burgundy had been established as a GERMANIC kingdom during the fifth century, its art being Germanic in character until the kingdom was absorbed into the CAROLINGIAN Empire. However, it is to a later phase in the history of the region that the term is generally applied in a cultural context.

In 1384 the Duchy of Burgundy and the county of Franche-Comté were united as a consequence of the marriage (1369) of Philip the Bold, Duke of Burgundy, and Margaret of Flanders (heiress to Franche-Comté). The union initiated a century of Burgundian greatness. Strategically placed as it was between France and Germany, Burgundy became the major Northern European political and economic power. The arts flowered under the patronage of Dukes Philip the Good (r. 1419–67) and Charles the Bold (r. 1467–77), who sought to create a dynastic culture. This period of creativity in the arts continued after the duchy's absorption into the Holy Roman Empire in 1477; indeed, it lasted well into the sixteenth century in the work of artists such as Simon Bening.

Books played a key role in Burgundian culture, with many illuminated CHRONICLES, ROMANCES, and devotional works being commissioned in Flanders, the center of Burgundian power. Burgundian patronage brought Flemish ILLUMINATION and SCRIPT (*lettre bourguignonne* or *bâtarde*) to international prominence with a luxurious, highly polished style. This style was influenced by the observation of court life and by contemporary Flemish panel painting, particularly the latter's rendering of space and use of opulent colors. David Aubert was an important SCRIBE within this milieu, and the many prominent illuminators included the MASTER of Mary of Burgundy, Simon Marmion, and Gerard Horenbout.

BURNISHING

Enhancing the smoothness and shininess of a surface such as metallic PIGMENT by polishing with a burnisher—a smooth, hard stone (such as agate), metal, or bone set into a handle. See also GILDING.

BYZANTINE

The Byzantine Empire is named for the ancient city of Byzantium, where Constantine the Great founded a new city, Constantinople, as the eastern capital of the Roman Empire in 330. Culturally the Byzantine Empire fused Greek, Roman, and Christian elements, though its language was Greek. The eastern Empire withstood the barbarian onslaught of the fifth century, but from the seventh century on suffered frequent invasions by Islamic forces.

The culture of Byzantium influenced the entire Greek world, including parts of Asia Minor as well as the regions of Italy with which it was politically and/or commercially engaged: Ravenna, the Veneto, southern Italy, and Sicily, where medieval art exhibited substantial Byzantine influence. Byzantine culture also spread northward when the Slavs, Russians, and other Central European groups converted to Christianity. The period of the Iconoclastic Controversy (726–843), during which many political and ecclesiastical leaders of the Byzantine Empire opposed the use of religious images, curbed the spread of Byzantine culture to the West. The schism that formed between the eastern and western Churches was most intense in the ninth and eleventh centuries.

There were, nevertheless, important phases of Byzantine influence on the West, notably during the OTTONIAN and parts of the ROMANESQUE periods. The Crusades of the eleventh to the thirteenth century, when Western European forces sought to recapture Jerusalem from the Islamic conquerors, again made Byzantine culture more accessible to the West, especially during the years of the Latin control of Byzantium (1204–61), following the Fourth Crusade. The TRANSITIONAL STYLE in Western art,

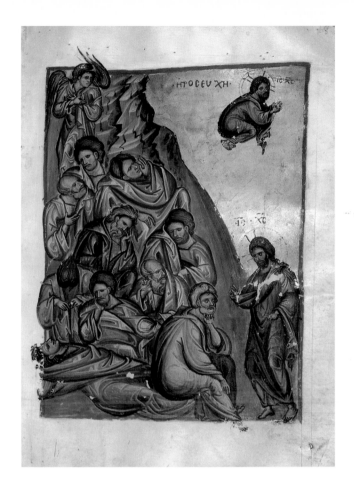

BYZANTINE

The Agony in the Garden.
Gospel book. Turkey
(Constantinople?), 13th
century. 20.5×15 cm
(8 1/16 × 5 7/8 in.). JPGM, Ms.
Ludwig II 5 (83.MB.69),
fol. 68.

from the late twelfth to the early thirteenth century, is a product
of this cultural interchange.

The Byzantine Empire itself enjoyed something of a golden
age from 850 to 1050, especially under the Macedonian emperors, accompanied by a flowering of the arts. During the fourteenth century, the Palaeologan dynasty (1258–1453) supported
culture and monasticism. In 1453, however, Constantinople fell to
the Ottoman Turks, and the Byzantine Empire came to an end.

Byzantine manuscript ILLUMINATION is characterized by an
iconic approach (see ICON), a relatively fixed ICONOGRAPHY of
biblical scenes, the use of flat gold backgrounds, but a generally
NATURALISTIC rendering of figures. At certain periods, however,
Byzantine illumination shows a tendency toward a MANNERED,
EXPRESSIONISTIC style. See also CHRYSOGRAPHY, COMPLEMENTARY
SHADING, and PURPLE PAGES.

The calendar sections of illuminated manuscripts most often precede liturgical and devotional texts. In this context, they identify feast days pertinent to the PATRON and the region, using different colors to highlight important feasts, such as Christmas or the Annunciation (so-called *red-letter days*). Calendars vary in accordance with local USE, and the deaths and saints' feasts commemorated often supply valuable evidence of ORIGIN and PROVENANCE. Private, university, and official administrative texts also included calendars, which enabled the literate community to calculate dates. Calendars were often illuminated, the two most popular schemes being the labors of the months (see OCCUPATIONAL CALENDAR) and the zodiacal signs, both ultimately of classical origin but increasingly popular from the ninth century on. Calendars

CALENDAR

Gerard Horenbout. *The Month of April.* Spinola Hours. Belgium (Ghent or Mechelen), c. 1515. 23.2 × 16.6 cm (9⅛ × 6 9⁄16 in.). JPGM, Ms. Ludwig IX 18 (83.ML.114), fol. 3.

The decoration of this calendar page includes a scene of herding (the labor of the month), Taurus (the appropriate zodiacal sign), and Saint Mark the Evangelist (whose feast day is April 25).

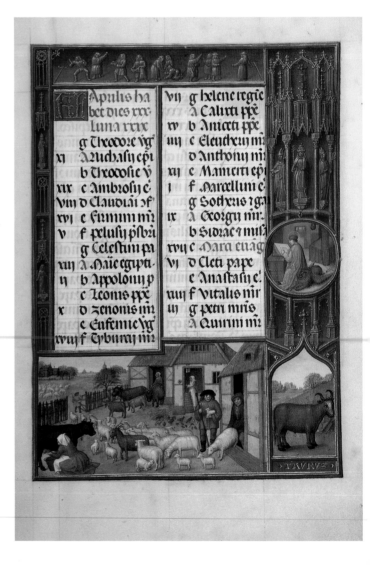

are often accompanied in religious books by devices for calculating movable feasts, such as Easter Tables. Medical and astronomical calendars appear in manuscripts relevant to those disciplines.

The Middle Ages inherited the Julian (Old Style) calendar introduced by Julius Caesar in 45 B.C. This contained a 365-day year, with an extra day every fourth year to reconcile the calendar with the solar year, calculated as 365 days and 6 hours. The year was divided into twelve months. Each month had named days: Kalends, Nones, and Ides, the unnamed days in between being reckoned backwards from the next Kalends, Nones, or Ides. Some months had *dies Aegyptiacae* ("Egyptian," or unlucky, days). Although commonly used, from EARLY CHRISTIAN times these Roman days competed with the ecclesiastical division of the year into weeks, each with seven named days, and with dating by reference to church feasts or occasions such as fairs and rent days.

The Roman civil year, beginning on January 1, continued to be used until the seventh century, when it was increasingly replaced by the Christian year, calculated from the year of Christ's birth, a system initially arising from the Dionysian Easter Table of c. 525 and popularized by the English scholar-theologian Bede during the eighth century. In this system Christmas, the Annunciation (March 25) or, less commonly, Easter marked the start of the year. Whatever the start of the year, the era began with the birth of Christ, the "year of grace."

Other calendrical styles were used in the Middle Ages as alternatives to or in association with the ecclesiastical "year of grace." Among these was the *indiction*, originally a civil reckoning that computed from 312 A.D. in fifteen-year cycles and was used for privileges and legal documents until relegated to notarial use in the late thirteenth century. Pontifical and regnal years also served calendrical purposes, relating a date to the person under whose jurisdiction the calendar was issued (for example, the second year of the reign of Henry III). Certain administrative offices had their own systems (the English Exchequer's financial year ran from Michaelmas, September 29, to Michaelmas). Spain, Portugal, and southwestern France used the Spanish Era calendar, beginning on January 1, 38 B.C., which survived in some areas until the fifteenth century.

The inclusion of devices such as the Golden Number, Epacts, Dominical letters, and Concurrents for the calculation of movable feasts (often added as tables) rendered a calendar perpetual or continually functional. The calculations were mostly concerned with establishing the relationship between the solar year and the phases of the moon so that the date of Easter could be determined. See also ASTRONOMICAL/ASTROLOGICAL TEXTS, COMPUTUS TEXTS, DIRECTORY, and MEDICAL TEXTS.

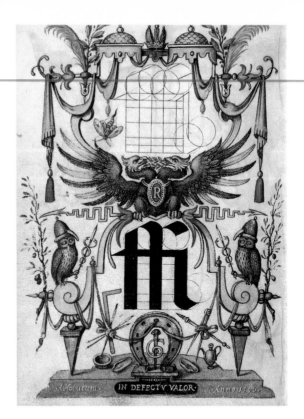

CALLIGRAPHY

From the Greek for "beautiful writing," calligraphy is a SCRIPT that exhibits exceptional and often self-conscious artistry and aesthetic quality in design and execution. The art of fine writing was appreciated during the Middle Ages and the RENAISSANCE, with certain SCRIBES becoming noted for their beautiful and decorative script. A number of treatises on calligraphy and specimen books of script (such as copy books and alphabet books) were produced. Following the introduction of printing, fine writing was still taught by writing masters, calligraphers, and ILLUMINATORS, who continued to produce handwritten pieces as works of art and for formal, commemorative, or display purposes. See also the illustration accompanying EPISTOLARY.

CAMPAIGN

A phase of work in the production of a manuscript. A manuscript could be made over a period of time in several campaigns of work; additional material might be added in a separate, later campaign.

CANONICAL HOURS

See DIVINE OFFICE.

CANON PAGE

See MISSAL.

A Gospel concordance system devised in the fourth century by Eusebius of Caesarea, in which Gospel passages are numbered in the text (generally in the margins) and correspond to tables, arranged in columnar form, indicating the concordance of passages among the Gospels. Canon tables were generally placed at the beginning of the book and were popular in GOSPEL BOOKS, BIBLES, and New Testaments (the Gospels plus Acts, Epistles, and Revelation), especially during the early Middle Ages. Canon tables were often set within arched surrounds of an architectural character. Sometimes EVANGELIST SYMBOLS were included to identify the Gospels referred to in the columns of numbers; these are known as *beast canon tables*.

Canon tables
Canon table page with symbols of the four evangelists ("beast canons"). Harley Golden Gospels. Germany (Aachen), c. 800. 36.5 × 25 cm (14⅜ × 9¹³⁄₁₆ in.). BL, Harley Ms. 2788, fol. 7.

Carolingian

The Carolingians were dynastic rulers of Frankia from 751, when Pepin the Short was named King of the Franks. The Carolingian Empire (which embraced much of Northern Europe and Italy) was established under Charlemagne (742–814), who became emperor in 800. In 843, the empire was divided into three parts by the Treaty of Verdun. The fragmentation of Charlemagne's realm continued, destroying any semblance of unity. Although

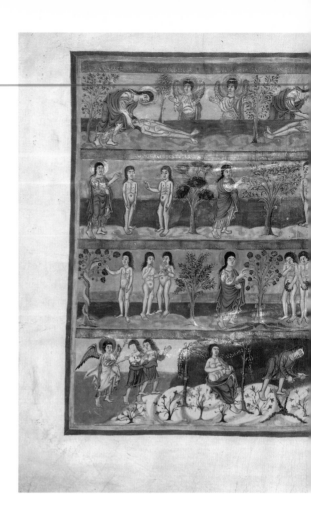

Carolingians ruled some areas until the late tenth century, the
OTTONIAN dynasty assumed imperial power in 962.

Charlemagne and his immediate successors sought to establish
cultural cohesion and political stability throughout the disparate
territories of the empire. This led to the flowering of culture
known as the *Carolingian renaissance* and to ecclesiastical reform.
The latter included the standardization of texts, for which reason
Charlemagne's adviser, Alcuin of York (c. 730–804), undertook a
revision of the BIBLE and the SACRAMENTARY. During the ninth
century, Alcuin's SCRIPTORIUM at Tours went on to produce large,
illuminated Bibles for circulation. The SCRIPT known as *Caroline
minuscule* was also part of the reform movement. Standardized
and easily legible, it was promoted throughout the Empire.

Charlemagne's claims to the imperial status of Roman emperors and his extension of Carolingian power into Italy fostered a
revival of CLASSICAL TEXTS and of the style and imagery of

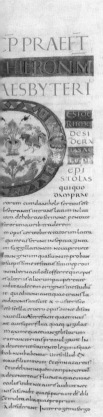

CAROLINGIAN

Scenes from the Creation and Fall of Humanity; text page with decorated initial *D*. Moutiers-Grandval Bible. France (Tours), c. 840. Leaf: 51 × 37.5 cm (20 1/16 × 14 3/4 in.). BL, Add. Ms. 10546, fols. 5v–6.

ancient art. Initially focused on the Court and Palace Schools at Aachen, the Carolingian renaissance was rapidly disseminated with the assistance of the Frankish bishops and their scriptoria (such as those at Corbie, Tours, Reims, and Metz). In addition to preserving many works from ANTIQUITY (see ASTRONOMICAL/ ASTROLOGICAL TEXTS and MEDICAL TEXTS), the Carolingian period witnessed the composition of many new texts by scholars such as Alcuin, Einhard, Paul the Deacon, Hrabanus Maurus, Walafrid Strabo, and John Scotus Eriugena.

The earliest monument of Carolingian ILLUMINATION, the Godescalc EVANGELARY, dates to c. 781–83; at this time, the scriptorium at Corbie was experimenting with early Caroline minuscule. The production of manuscripts flourished until the late ninth century, with a number of distinctive local styles emerging. The Court School of Charlemagne, for example, favored heavily painted works with a NATURALISTIC rendering of figures and opulent use of gold, silver, and purple (redolent of imperial Roman and BYZANTINE influence). The artists of the School of Reims worked in an agitated, IMPRESSIONISTIC style of classical inspiration, while illuminators of the Metz School employed a decorative style with much feathery ACANTHUS ornament. During the ninth century, the Franco-Saxon style also emerged, showing INSULAR influence in its zoomorphic and INTERLACE decoration. Carolingian book production was also influenced by PRE-CAROLINGIAN European developments. See also the illustration accompanying CANON TABLES.

CARPET PAGE

An ornamental page particularly favored in INSULAR art, sometimes incorporating a cross into its design, that derives its name from its visual similarity to an Eastern carpet. Unlike decorated INCIPIT PAGES, carpet pages do not carry text. They generally separated the four Gospels in a manuscript, and their use in Christian art may be of COPTIC origin. See the illustration accompanying INSULAR.

CARTOLAIO
(pl. CARTOLAI)

See STATIONER.

CARTOUCHE

An ornament in the form of a scroll or shield.

CARTULARY

A collection of CHARTERS in book form.

CATCHWORD

A word written at the end (generally in the lower margin) of a QUIRE that repeats the first word on the following page. Catchwords facilitate the arrangement of the quires during binding. They were introduced into Europe via Spain, Italy, and southwest France around 1000, possibly under Islamic influence.

CELTIC

The Celts were originally an Iron Age people, occupying Central and Western Europe, whose culture spread throughout much of the West. Following Roman expansionism of the first century B.C. to the first century A.D., the Celts were pushed back to areas of the Atlantic seaboard (Ireland, Scotland, Man, Wales, Cornwall, and Brittany). Celtic art is characterized by a sophisticated abstract approach, featuring devices such as the *pelta* (a triangle with one convex and two concave sides), the *trumpet spiral* (a spiral with an expanded triangular mouth), and the *triquetra* (a triple loop formed of intersecting arcs) and often incorporates anthropomorphic and zoomorphic features, sometimes of an ambiguous character. "Ultimate La Tène" art, named after a Celtic Iron Age style, flourishes even to the present.

Beginning in the fifth century, Ireland, along with some other areas of Celtic Britain, developed a thriving literate Christian tradition and played a key role in preserving the learning of ANTIQUITY and the early Church. This was transmitted to ANGLO-SAXON England from the sixth century on, giving rise to INSULAR culture. Following the Viking incursions of the ninth century, Celtic culture became increasingly independent of Anglo-Saxon culture. See the illustration accompanying INSULAR.

CHAINED BOOK

A book whose BINDING carries a STAPLE and chain for attachment to a desk or lectern, on which the book was read. The presence of a staple and chain generally denotes institutional ownership by a college or ecclesiastical establishment (for example, the chained library at Hereford Cathedral).

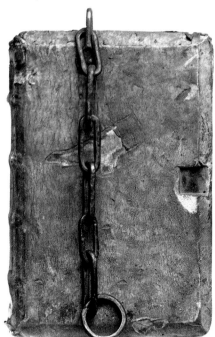

CHAINED BOOK
Front cover. John Sintram, Collection of moralized exempla. Germany (Würzburg), early 15th century. 22.3 × 15 cm (8¾ × 5⅞ in.). BL, Add. Ms. 44055.

CHALK

Chiefly composed of calcium carbonate, chalk was used for a variety of purposes in manuscript production: as a POUNCE when preparing the PARCHMENT surface; as a component of GESSO or another GROUND; as a white PIGMENT; as an alkaline component in pigments (serving to modify the color of certain organic pigments, such as folium, and to lighten and increase the opacity of others); or as a drawing medium.

CHANNELING

A system of grooves cut into binding BOARDS to carry the CORDS that attach the boards to the QUIRES. The use of channels meant that the cords would not stand proud on the inside of the boards. See also PEGGING.

CHANNEL SCHOOL

A SCHOOL OF ILLUMINATION that flourished in England and northern France in the eleventh and twelfth centuries. The term emphasizes the close stylistic relationship between works produced on either side of the English Channel. INSULAR art had already exerted a formative influence on northern French ILLUMINATION in the ninth century (see CAROLINGIAN) and had in turn begun to absorb French influences. After the introduction of Norman artists and SCRIBES into England following the Norman Conquest in 1066, this trend increased, contributing to the development of ROMANESQUE art.

CHARTER

A document recording a juridical act, most commonly the grant of property or of rights relating to property.

CHEMISE BINDING

The medieval precursor of the modern dust jacket, a chemise is a slip-on cover of leather or of a textile such as velvet or linen that protected the BINDING of a book and its FORE EDGE. Chemises varied in form from high-grade luxurious embellishments for BOOKS OF HOURS and PRAYER BOOKS to functional wrappers for administrative records and library books.

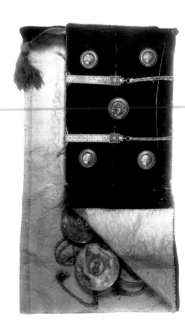

CHEMISE BINDING
Chemise of velvet, silk, and gold, with silver seal boxes. Book of charters of the reign of King Henry VII of England. England, c. 1500. 70×30 cm (27⁹⁄₁₆×11¹³⁄₁₆ in.). BL, Harley Ms. 1498.

CHI-RHO

A monogram composed of the letters XP (the Greek *chi* and *rho*), the first two characters of the name of Christ in Greek. It was often used as a symbol in EARLY CHRISTIAN art and life. Decorated chi-rho pages are found in early medieval GOSPEL BOOKS, at Matthew 1:18.

CHOIR BOOK

A SERVICE BOOK containing the parts of the MASS or the DIVINE OFFICE sung by the choir. See also MUSIC MANUSCRIPTS.

CHRONICLE

A collection of annals or notes of yearly events. Such recordings developed from the practice of annotating Easter Tables (see CALENDAR). Early chronicles took the form of world or universal histories, such as those written in the fourth century by Eusebius of Caesarea and Sulpicius Severus. Local chronicles began to appear in the ninth century; among the most notable are the *Annals of Ulster*, the *Frankish Royal Annals*, the *Anglo-Saxon Chronicle*, and a history of the Saxon kings by the German bishop Thietmar of Merseburg in the early eleventh century. World chronicles continued to be written, however, perpetuated by historians such as Marianus Scotus in the later eleventh century. The *Historia ecclesiastica*, completed in 731 at Jarrow in northeastern England by the Venerable Bede, marked an influential new approach to the writing of history: Bede perceived a relationship of cause and effect between events, collated material in accordance with a central theme (the growth of Christianity in England), and promoted a consistent system of dating (from the Incarnation).

The Normans produced a number of historical works relating to Normandy, England, and the Holy Land in the later eleventh and twelfth centuries; these include the *Gesta Normannorum ducum* of William of Jumièges, the *Gesta Guillelmi ducis Normannorum et regis Anglorum* of William of Poitiers, and the works of Sigebert of Gembloux, Robert of Torigni, and Ordericus Vitalis. History writing in Britain continued to proliferate throughout the twelfth and thirteenth centuries, with chronicles by Florence of Worcester, William of Malmesbury, Geoffrey of Monmouth, Giraldus Cambrensis, and Matthew Paris. Important Continental historians of the thirteenth century include Salimbene (*Cronica*) and Vincent of Beauvais (*Speculum historiale*), the latter representing a move toward a more encyclopedic world view. Histories based on the BIBLE, such as the thirteenth-century *Weltchronik* of Rudolf von Ems, were also compiled. The thirteenth century also witnessed a proliferation of VERNACULAR histories, among them Villehardouin's *Conquête de Constantinople*, the *Histoire de Guillaume le Maréchal*, the *Grandes Chroniques françaises de Saint-Denis*, Jean Creton's *Histoire de Roy d'Angleterre Richard*, and Jean Froissart's *Chroniques*

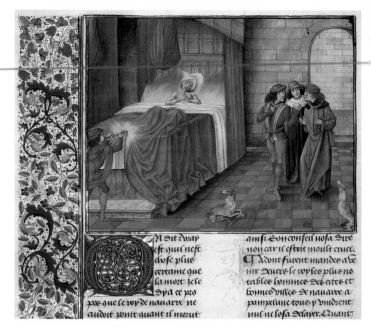

de France, d'Engleterre et des païs voisins, the last representing a
fusion of the traditional chronicle with the ROMANCE genre.

During the GOTHIC period, many historical works were illustrated, a practice largely initiated by Giraldus Cambrensis and
Matthew Paris, who incorporated marginal drawings into some of
their works. In the thirteenth century, some authors attempted to
integrate pagan and Christian history by grafting books such as
Peter of Poitiers' *Genealogy of Christ* onto universal chronicles. The
genealogies of kings were also included, giving rise to a tradition
of illuminated genealogical manuscripts, often in ROLL form.

CHRYSOGRAPHY

From the Greek word *chrysographia*, meaning "writing in gold,"
chrysography is the use of powdered gold, mixed with glair or
gum (see BINDING MEDIUM) to create an INK; when dry, the ink is
usually burnished (see BURNISHING). Gold (and silver) writing on
PARCHMENT is known from the EARLY CHRISTIAN period on. PUR-
PLE PAGES were introduced in BYZANTINE books at least as early as
the sixth century as a more suitable and luxurious background for
such SCRIPT; the imperial connotation of having been "born to the
purple" was implicit in the ostentatious use of the color. Chrysography was practiced in INSULAR, ANGLO-SAXON, CAROLINGIAN,
and OTTONIAN luxury book production and also occurs sporadically later in the Middle Ages and the RENAISSANCE. Gold ink was
also used in Byzantine ILLUMINATION to provide highlights (especially in articulating drapery) and other details, a technique transmitted to the West, where it enjoyed particular popularity during

the fifteenth century. Chrysography in late GOTHIC art is often somewhat formulaic and mechanical, but it achieved great refinement in panel painting and within RENAISSANCE illumination.

CLAREA

See BINDING MEDIUM.

CLASP

A metal fitting attached to the BOARDS at the FORE EDGE of a BINDING in order to hold the book shut and to preserve the PARCHMENT (unless kept at an appropriate temperature and humidity level, parchment tends to cockle and return to the original shape of the animal skin). Clasps became popular during the fourteenth century (alongside their earlier counterpart, the STRAP AND PIN), initially as a combination of metal fittings and leather straps and then entirely of metal. On English and some French bindings the clasps fasten at the lower board, while elsewhere on the Continent the catch is on the upper board.

CLASSICAL TEXTS

Literary works of Greek and Roman ANTIQUITY. Despite their pagan ancestry, a wide range of classical texts was preserved during the early Middle Ages, including works by authors such as Dioscorides, Pliny the Elder, Cicero, Sextus Placitus, and Vitruvius, in fields ranging from medicine to rhetoric. Parts of Italy, Spain, and Gaul as well as the INSULAR and ANGLO-SAXON worlds did much to preserve classical learning, while the CAROLINGIAN renaissance promoted a conscious reference to and revival of antique works. Islam also became the custodian of a significant body of classical texts, notably the works of Plato, Aristotle, Galen of Pergamon, and Hippocrates, which it transmitted to the West beginning in the twelfth century, contributing to the rise of scholasticism. The RENAISSANCE again witnessed a revival and systematic rediscovery of the classical past in the work of the humanists (see HUMANISTIC). Several cycles of illustration were also inherited from classical texts (see ASTRONOMICAL/ASTROLOGICAL TEXTS, BESTIARY, HERBAL, and MEDICAL TEXTS).

CLASSICIZING

A classicizing style emulates the form or character of the art of classical ANTIQUITY.

CLOTHLET

A piece of cloth impregnated with PIGMENT (generally a vegetable dye). A portion of such cloth, when soaked in a little BINDING MEDIUM, releases its colorant and produces an artist's pigment. Clothlets are called *petiae* in Latin and *pezze* or *pezzette* in Italian; *bisetus folii* refers to clothlets dyed with folium, or turnsole, extract. Clothlets were a convenient way of carrying or shipping vegetal pigments, and they were especially popular from the fourteenth century on, with the growth of the textile trade. Glazes of vegetal dyes were often used to enhance other colors in book ILLUMINATION, since they created a rich, glowing, and transparent effect.

CODEX
(pl. CODICES)

Originating in the first century, the codex (from *caudex*, the Latin word for tree bark) is a book composed of folded sheets sewn along one edge, distinct from other writing vehicles such as the ROLL or TABLET. The codex was initially a low-grade form manufactured of PAPYRUS. Its portability and ease of consultation made it popular among Christians. Following the Christianization of the Roman Empire in the fourth century, the codex supplanted the roll as the favored vehicle for literary texts.

CODICOLOGY

The study of the physical structure of the book, which promotes a better understanding of its production and subsequent history. The term was initially coined in 1943 in relation to the listing of texts in catalogue form but was subsequently applied to book structures. From the late nineteenth century on, advances in the study of book structures led to the formulation of certain guidelines for reconstructing their historical development, since such structures vary with time and place. Variable features include the number of leaves used in a QUIRE, the relative disposition of the HAIR and FLESH SIDES of the PARCHMENT, the manner of PRICKING and RULING (and whether these processes were conducted before or after the leaves were folded, one or more leaves at a time, or with the aid of a template), and how a book was sewn and bound. The examination of a book's structure can shed considerable light on its method of construction, place of ORIGIN, and PROVENANCE and can help to reconstruct its original appearance. See also COLLATION, ILLUMINATOR, MONASTIC PRODUCTION, PALEOGRAPHY, PECIA SYSTEM, SCRIBE, SECULAR PRODUCTION, and STATIONER.

COLLATION

A description of a book's current and original structure, that is, the arrangement of its leaves and QUIRES. This information may be conveyed in diagrammatic form (showing the quires and their composition) or in a prose shorthand. In the latter, for example, "1⁸ (wants 1, blank)" indicates that the first quire was formed of eight leaves, the first of which is missing and was probably originally blank. Two collations may be given to indicate differences between a book's current and original structures, but a single collation can often convey data relevant to both states.

COLLECTAR

A SERVICE BOOK containing the collects (or prayers) for the canonical hours of the DIVINE OFFICE. Such volumes often also contain *capitula* (short selections from Scripture read after the Psalms) and may open with a CALENDAR.

COLOPHON

An inscription recording information relating to the circumstances of the production of a manuscript or printed book (the place and/or people involved and, less frequently, the date). Colophons appear only sporadically in medieval books, but were often employed by the Italian humanists (see HUMANISTIC), who also included the date. They are generally located at the end of a book. The term is also used to designate the emblem or DEVICE of a publishing house.

COLOPHON DECORATION

Simple decorative devices, such as dots, commas, ivy leaves (*hedera*), or box surrounds, which serve to highlight the COLOPHON. Such decoration is found in ANTIQUITY and EARLY CHRISTIAN manuscripts.

COLUMN PICTURE

A MINIATURE that occupies the width of a column (but not necessarily its height).

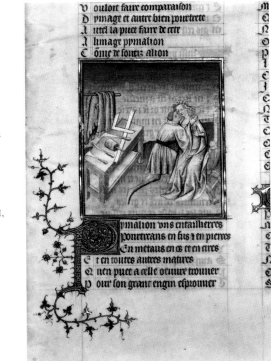

COLUMN PICTURE
Master of the Roman de la Rose. *Pygmalion and Galatea.* Guillaume de Lorris and Jean de Meun, *Roman de la rose.* France (Paris), c. 1405. 36.7 × 26 cm (14⁷⁄₁₆ × 10¼ in.). JPGM, Ms. Ludwig XV 7 (83.MR.177), fol. 130 (detail).

COMMENTARY

A discussion and/or expansion of a text, generally of a biblical, PATRISTIC, or legal character. Commentaries often accompanied the texts they discussed in the form of GLOSSES. See the illustration accompanying DECRETALS.

COMPLEMENTARY SHADING

The practice, BYZANTINE in origin, of rendering shading in the modeling of a figure or drapery in a complementary (that is, contrasting) color, rather than with a darker shade of the same color or with black. The technique often produces an image of greater NATURALISTIC as well as decorative effect.

COMPUTUS TEXTS

Works dealing with the calculation of time. These include CALENDARS, Easter Tables, almanacs, and other ASTRONOMICAL/ASTROLOGICAL TEXTS, as well as specific treatises such as the Venerable Bede's *De temporum ratione* of 725. Manuscripts of computus texts often include diagrams and even figural decoration. See also VADE MECUM and VOLVELLE.

CONJOINT

Conjoint (or conjugate) leaves are two leaves that are or were part of the same BIFOLIUM.

CONTINUATION PANEL

Like a DISPLAY PANEL, a continuation panel provides a decorative background or frame to the letters following a major INITIAL; these latter are known as *continuation lettering*.

COPTIC

A Copt is a native Egyptian descended from the ancient Egyptians. Following the Arab conquest of 640, the term (Arabic *qibt*, derived from the Greek *aiguptios*) was used to refer to the indigenous population of Egypt, which was predominantly Christian. By the sixteenth century, Westerners used it to distinguish Christian inhabitants from the Muslim majority. The Coptic Church exerted an influence on the West from the sixth to the eighth century, especially in the field of eremitic monasticism, and may have contributed certain features to book production, such as COPTIC SEWING and ornamental CARPET PAGES.

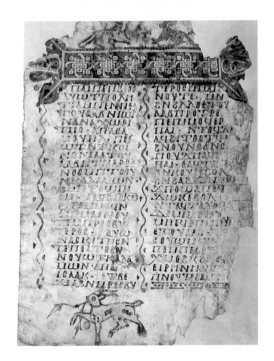

COPTIC

Text page with decorated headpiece. Leaf from *Life of Saint Samuel*, in Coptic. Egypt (probably Tutun), 10th century. 34.9×25.4 cm (13¾×10 in.). JPGM, Ms. 12 (85.MS.119).

COPTIC SEWING

A method (with several variants) of SEWING a book during BINDING: the QUIRES are sewn together by thread carried by two needles working in a figure-eight movement from quire to quire. The BOARDS are then laced onto the loose ends of these threads. Coptic, or *unsupported*, sewing is unlike SEWING ON SUPPORTS, the technique usually employed in the medieval West, in that the quires are not linked by sewing onto CORDS.

Coptic sewing, which provides a more flexible BINDING and facilitates opening the CODEX, is generally found in Egyptian and some other Eastern bindings. Among the rare surviving examples from the medieval West is the Stonyhurst, or Cuthbert, Gospel, an INSULAR Gospel of Saint John made at Monkwearmouth/Jarrow in the late seventh century for placement in the coffin of Saint Cuthbert.

CORDS

The horizontal supporting bands onto which QUIRES are sewn at the SPINE to form the book. Cords are generally bands of leather (or sometimes other materials such as hemp) and could appear in single or double form; in the latter, the cords are split along most of their length to allow a double, figure-eight sewing around them for additional strength. The ends of the cords are then threaded into the BOARDS (see CHANNELING and PEGGING) and the structure covered. The cords appear as raised bands when seen through the covering of the spine, but beginning in the later sixteenth century could fit into grooves "sawn-in" to the quire to produce a flatter spine. See also SEWING ON SUPPORTS and SEWING STATIONS.

CORNERPIECE Cornerpieces are metal plaques attached to the corners of the BOARDS of a BINDING to protect them, a popular feature from the fifteenth century on. The term also refers to a decorative motif in the corners of a MINIATURE or BORDER.

CORRECTION Corrections to a text were undertaken by the SCRIBE, another member of the SCRIPTORIUM, a STATIONER, an owner, or a subsequent reader. They take various forms, including simple interlinear or marginal insertions (perhaps marked by a SIGNE-DE-RENVOI), erasures made by scraping with a KNIFE or PUMICE (or washing, in the case of PAPYRUS), cancellations indicated by crossing out, or expunctuation (in which points placed beneath a letter or word mark its deletion). Some corrections resulted from a systematic program of comparing a text against another copy; others represent the independent decision of a scribe or reader to amend words or passages. The process of correction frequently formed part of the production of a manuscript.

CRAYON A stick of white or colored CHALK or other solidified PIGMENT, sometimes contained in a holder, used for drawing, annotation, and occasionally for RULING.

CUSTOMARY A book describing the customs—the rituals accompanying liturgical services or monastic discipline, for example—of an ecclesiastical establishment. A customary is a form of DIRECTORY and is also known as a *consuetudinary* or *Liber ordinarius*.

CUT LEATHER A technique for decorating BINDING in which the leather of a cover is cut away with a knife to leave a picture or design in relief. Cut-leather decoration was practiced primarily in German-speaking countries from the late fourteenth to the early sixteenth century. See also TOOLED.

CUTTING A piece, often a MINIATURE or painted INITIAL, cut out of a manuscript, generally for commercial or collecting purposes. Cuttings were frequently collected for their independent aesthetic value, especially during the nineteenth century. See the illustration accompanying MINIATURE.

DAMP FOLD A term coined in the mid-twentieth century to refer to a style of depicting drapery in which the material appears to cling to the body like wet cloth. The drapery folds not only articulate the human figure but, being sinuous and rhythmical, produce a decorative effect. The style ultimately derives from BYZANTINE art, but is found in the West from the twelfth century on and is an international feature of ROMANESQUE art. Three variations of damp-fold drapery have been noted: a style composed of concentric lines, particularly favored in Burgundy in the twelfth century; *nested V* folds, in which planes of drapery of ovoid or pear shape terminate in a series of V's—a widespread convention for rendering hanging drapery; the *clinging curvilinear* style, characterized by S-shaped lines, which enjoyed its greatest popularity in England, becoming something of a hallmark of English art around 1140–70. This latter style is often termed the *Bury Bible figure style* after one of its earliest and most important representatives. See the illustration accompanying ROMANESQUE.

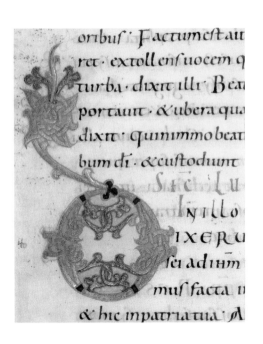

DECORATED INITIAL
Decorated initial *D*. Evangelary. Germany or Switzerland (Reichenau or St. Gall), late 10th century. 27.7 × 19.1 cm (10⅞ × 7½ in.). JPGM, Ms. 16 (85.MD.317), fol. 33 (detail).

DECORATED INITIAL

An INITIAL composed of non-figural, non-zoomorphic decorative elements.

DECORATED LETTER

See INITIAL.

DECRETALS

Decretals are collections of letters containing papal rulings of local or universal application, often made in response to an appeal and frequently relating to matters of canonical discipline. Decretals may be illuminated with scenes germane to the text or with scenes designed to relieve the text, such as BAS-DE-PAGE scenes narrating

SAINTS' LIVES or amusing scenes from daily life and GROTESQUES. Copies of decretals were often required by ecclesiastical and civil authorities or for study purposes in universities, notably those specializing in law, such as the university at Bologna.

The earliest decretals were simple collections of papal letters. They were often included in collections of canon law and as early as the fifth century were themselves arranged in collections. Among the most notable are: the *Collectio Dionysiana* of Dionysius Exiguus, compiled c. 514; Pope Hadrian I's collection, sent to Charlemagne in 774 (*Collectio Dionysio-Hadriana*), which became the authoritative Frankish text on canon law; the Spanish sixth-century collection associated with Isidore of Seville (*Hispana collectio*); the *False Decretals of Pseudo-Isidore*, compiled in France around 850; the ninth-century Italian *Anselmo dedicata collectio*; the tenth-century *Collectio* of Abbo of Fleury; Regino of Prüm's collection of canon laws made in 906; the *Decretum* of Burchard of Worms, c. 1012, an influential collection designed to promote church

DECRETALS

Text page with *A Wild Man Seizing a Woman* (in the bas-de-page). Smithfield Decretals (the decretals of Pope Gregory IX with a gloss by Bernard of Parma). Written in Italy and illuminated in England (London?), early 14th century. 45 × 28 cm (17 11/16 × 11 in.). BL, Royal Ms. 10.E.IV, fol. 72.

reorganization; and the late eleventh-century *Decretum* of Ivo of Chartres. Gratian's *Decretum* of c. 1140 summarized older letters and conciliar decrees and became the most important law book of the twelfth century. It marked the end of the traditional form of collection, giving rise to the greatest period of legal scholarship in the Roman Church. Later collections include the *Quinque compilationes antiquae*; the *Decretals* of Pope Gregory IX of 1234, an important new edition of canon law; the *Liber sextus* of Pope Boniface VIII of 1298; and the *Constitutiones Clementinae* of Pope Clement V of 1317. Decretals generated a number of COMMENTARIES, which often appeared as GLOSSES.

DEDICATION MINIATURE See PRESENTATION MINIATURE.

DEVICE A figure or design, often accompanied by a MOTTO, used to identify an individual, family, or nation. See also EMBLEM and HERALDRY.

DIAPER PATTERN From the French *diapré* ("variegated"), a diaper pattern is a repetitive geometric pattern. Although used as early as the eleventh century, it often acted as a background in GOTHIC illumination. Some artists even seem to have specialized in diaper grounds.

DIGEST A compilation of legal rules and statutes. The earliest digests were systematic, comprehensive treatises on Roman law, composed by classical Roman jurists. Medieval copies of these Roman digests were sometimes GLOSSED and illuminated, either with scenes related to the text or of an extraneous and often amusing character.

In December 530, the BYZANTINE Emperor Justinian ordered a team led by Tribonian to compile a collection of excerpts from the classical jurists. The resultant work was called the *Digest* (or *Pandects*). The *Digest*, which formed part of the larger Code of Justinian, was arranged in fifty books and subdivided by titles. During the Middle Ages, it was commonly divided into the *Digestum vetus* (books I–XXIV, 2), the *Infortiatum* (books XXIV, 2–XXXVIII), and the *Digestum novum* (books XXXIX–L).

DIMENSIONS When measuring a manuscript, the height of a leaf is given first, then the width. Manuscripts were often trimmed at some point in their history, and it is therefore useful to give the dimensions of the written space—the text block—as well. The FRAME RULING can conveniently be measured for this purpose. The metric system is preferred, with dimensions usually given in millimeters.

DIMINUENDO

A decorative device that makes the transition in scale from an enlarged INITIAL to the main SCRIPT used for the text. A diminuendo is accomplished by gradually reducing the height of a few letters following the initial. The device was particularly popular with INSULAR scribes.

DIPLOMATIC

Used as a noun, diplomatic refers to the study of documents and records, their form, language, and SCRIPT. The term was coined in the seventeenth century and initially embraced PALEOGRAPHY and CODICOLOGY.

DIRECTORY

A book containing aids or guidelines to assist in the performance of the LITURGY (including CALENDARS, CUSTOMARIES, and ORDINALS).

DISPLAY PANEL

A decorative panel containing DISPLAY SCRIPT.

DISPLAY SCRIPT

Decorative SCRIPT, generally incorporating higher grade letter forms and sometimes employing a variety of colors. Display script is often used, along with an enlarged INITIAL, to emphasize major textual openings. See the illustration accompanying INSULAR.

DIURNAL

A book, sometimes called a journal, used in the performance of the DIVINE OFFICE, but containing only the daytime offices (lauds, prime, terce, sext, none, and vespers). Its layout is like that of the BREVIARY or ANTIPHONAL, and its text varies in accordance with USE. The Nocturnal performs a similar function for the night offices.

DIVINE OFFICE

A cycle of daily devotions—the prayers of the canonical hours—performed by members of religious orders and the clergy. It originated in the services of the Jewish synagogue and in the Apostolic Church. Initially, each office consisted mainly of the recitation of Psalms and lessons from Scripture. In the fourth century, under the influence of Saint Ambrose, hymns and antiphons were added; one hundred and fifty years later, under Saint Benedict, there appeared responsories, canticles, collects, and other elaborations. By the eighth century, the cycle of eight canonical hours for the performance of the Divine Office had been fixed: matins (approximately 2:30 am), lauds (approximately 5 am), prime (approximately 6 am), terce (approximately 9 am), sext (approximately 12 noon), none (approximately 3 pm), vespers (approximately 4:30 pm), and compline (approximately 6 pm).

The Divine Office was initially arranged so that the complete PSALTER could be recited each week, and much of Holy Scripture throughout the year. During the Middle Ages, however, the celebration of saints' feast days and readings from their lives (see MARTYROLOGY) interfered with this structure, stimulating attempts at reform in the sixteenth century. Along with the MASS, the Divine Office forms the basis of Christian LITURGY. For a LAY response to the office, see BOOK OF HOURS.

DONOR

A person who donates a book—and often commissions it as well—to an ecclesiastical establishment. It is sometimes possible to identify the donor or owner of a book through the presence of an inscription, armorial bearings in images or margins, patron saint, or a MOTTO. Portraits of the donor (often STYLIZED, although some true portrait likenesses do occur) are found throughout the Middle Ages, but became increasingly popular from the thirteenth century on. Such portraits might show the donor kneeling before the Virgin and Child, or receiving or presenting the commissioned work. See also PATRON and the illustration accompanying LECTIONARY.

DRAFTSMAN

The person responsible for laying out a design, who may or may not be the artist responsible for the actual painting.

DROLLERY

An amusing figure, often of a GROTESQUE character. Drolleries appear throughout the history of book ILLUMINATION, from INSULAR works such as the Book of Kells to late medieval manuscripts

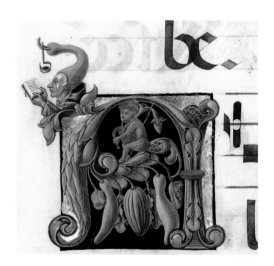

such as the PRAYER BOOK of Charles the Bold, but they were particularly popular from the thirteenth to the fifteenth century.

DRY POINT See HARD POINT.

EARLY CHRISTIAN

The Early Christian period extends from Apostolic times to around 600, when Pope Gregory the Great (c. 540–604) established a strong, independent Western Church that began the transition into the Middle Ages. The culture of the early BYZANTINE Empire is included under this heading. The Early Christian period (which overlapped with the LATE ANTIQUE) witnessed the beginnings of substantial book decoration: illuminated copies of the works of classical authors (such as the Roman Virgil) and of biblical texts (such as the Vienna Genesis and the Ashburnham PENTATEUCH) survive.

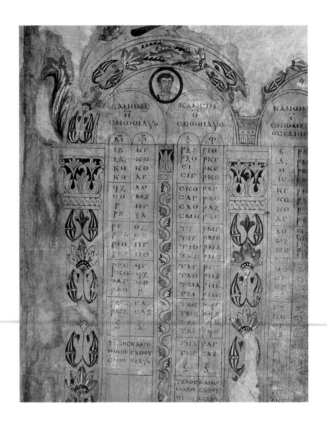

EARLY CHRISTIAN
Canon table page.
Gospel book. Turkey
(Constantinople), late 6th
or early 7th century.
22 × 15.8 cm (8¹¹⁄₁₆ × 6¼
in.). BL, Add. Ms. 5111,
fol. 11.

The canon tables of this
manuscript are written on
gold-stained parchment.

EMBLEM

(pl. EMBLEMATA)

A pictorial ALLEGORY or symbolic representation, often accompanied by a MOTTO. An emblem can serve as an identifying sign for a person, family, or nation.

Endbands are bands placed at the HEAD and TAIL of the SPINE of a book in order to consolidate its ends, strengthen the attachment of the BOARDS, and impede the entry of worms. They consist of cores generally of ALUM TAWED leather, hemp, PARCHMENT, or linen cord (with cane and rolled PAPER also used at later dates) and are usually covered by silk or thread embroidery, with highly varied patterns and techniques. Ideally, the endbands should be tied down in the centers of the QUIRES (often at the same point as the KETTLE STITCH) and their ends laced into the BINDING boards (see CHANNELING). The identification of different details of end-band sewing technique and patterning may help us group books together and assign them to specific production centers.

ENDPAPERS

Two or more blank or decorated leaves at the beginning or end of a book that can either line the BOARDS (fulfilling the function of PASTEDOWNS or decorative doublures) or serve as FLYLEAVES.

EPISTOLARY

A SERVICE BOOK containing the Epistle readings for the MASS arranged according to the liturgical year. The Epistle reading is

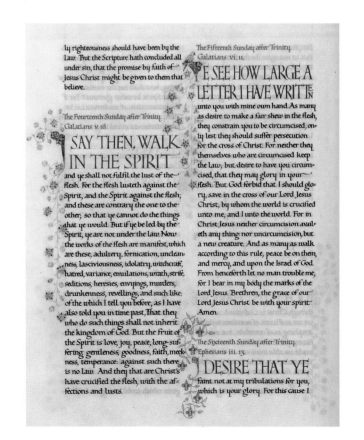

EPISTOLARY
Madelyn Walker. Text page. Epistolary. England, c. 1930. 36.4 × 25.3 cm (14³⁄₁₆ × 9¹⁵⁄₁₆ in.). JPGM, Ms. Ludwig IV 3 (83.ME.75), fol. 11v.

generally taken from the New Testament Epistles, but is sometimes drawn from other New and Old Testament Books. Epistle lists (*capitulare lectionum*) were very occasionally attached to BIBLES or to New Testament volumes. They listed the readings for the various feast days by opening words, again according to the liturgical year. At high mass the Epistle was read by a subdeacon.

EVANGELARY/ EVANGELISTARY

Also known as a Gospel LECTIONARY or pericope book, an evangelary contains the Gospel readings for the MASS, arranged according to the liturgical year. Since an evangelary gives the full reading (pericope) for each feast, and the pericopes are in liturgical order, it is a more practical volume to use in the celebration of mass than a GOSPEL BOOK with added capitularies. The evangelary became increasingly popular from the CAROLINGIAN period on.

EVANGELIST PORTRAIT

The evangelists are the "authors" of the Gospels (Matthew, Mark, Luke, and John). They were often depicted as SCRIBES from the EARLY CHRISTIAN period on. The rendering of their figures is often accompanied by, or conflated with, the EVANGELIST SYMBOLS. Other types of depictions of the evangelists include scenes of Saint John on Patmos (found in manuscripts of the Book of Revelation, or APOCALYPSE) and of Saint Luke making a portrait of the Virgin and Child (an image ultimately of BYZANTINE derivation, which is encountered most often in BOOKS OF HOURS).

EVANGELIST SYMBOL

Symbols of the evangelists derived from the Old Testament visions of Ezekiel and the vision of Saint John in the APOCALYPSE. In the West, the beasts of Saint John's vision are usually associated with the evangelists as follows: Matthew is represented by a man; Mark by a lion; Luke by a bull; and John by an eagle. The symbols may appear alone, either with ATTRIBUTES (wings, haloes, and books) or without ("terrestrial" symbols); they may identify accompanying EVANGELIST PORTRAITS; or they may be conflated with human figures to form zoo-anthropomorphic evangelist symbols.

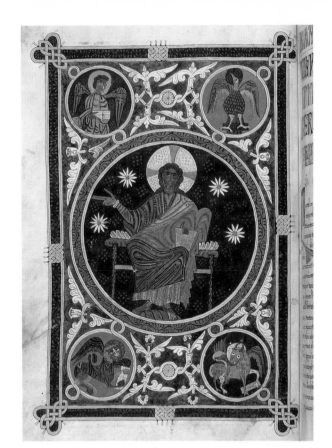

EXEMPLAR

A book from which another is copied. See also MODEL and PECIA SYSTEM.

EX LIBRIS INSCRIPTION

An inscription that records a book's inclusion in a library, whether private or institutional. Such inscriptions offer valuable evidence of a manuscript's PROVENANCE. Bookplates also carry ex libris information. Libraries often employed distinctive labeling and shelving systems, many of which have been identified, and such storage data also provide evidence of provenance.

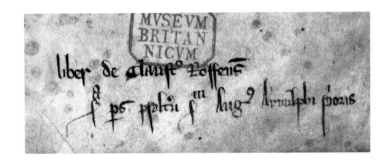

EXPLICIT

The closing of a textual unit, from the Latin *explicitus*, meaning "unrolled." When cataloguing manuscripts, the INCIPIT and explicit of a text are often cited to aid textual identification.

EXPRESSIONISTIC

An expressionistic style of painting is one that conveys a sense of heightened emotionality. This often entails a MANNERED or exaggerated treatment of forms. An expressionistic approach was especially prevalent in phases of BYZANTINE and English art and in German ILLUMINATION.

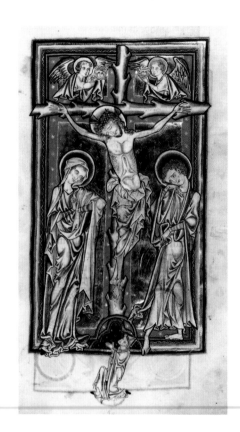

EXPRESSIONISTIC
The Crucifixion. Evesham Psalter. England (Worcester region), c. 1250–60. 31.5 × 21 cm (12⅜ × 8¼ in.). BL, Add. Ms. 44874, fol. 6.

EXULTET ROLL

See ROLL.

FLEMISH

See BURGUNDIAN.

FLESH SIDE

The side of a sheet of PARCHMENT or vellum that originally faced the animal's flesh. This is generally whiter and softer than the HAIR SIDE. The two sides are often readily distinguishable, save in INSULAR manuscripts, where skins were not scraped down as far, so that both sides retain a suedelike surface and sometimes a stiff, cellulose character.

FLYLEAF

Flyleaves at the beginning or end of a book serve to protect the text in the event of worming or damage to the BINDING. They often carry PEN TRIALS and INSCRIPTIONS concerning PROVENANCE. Flyleaves were sometimes used for trying out designs (see MODEL BOOK). See also ENDPAPERS and PASTEDOWN.

FOLIO

A sheet of writing material, one half of a BIFOLIUM. The front and back of a folio are referred to as the RECTO and VERSO, respectively. The numbering of leaves, as opposed to pages, is termed *foliation* and is commonly found in manuscripts. "Folio" and "folios" (or "folia") are often abbreviated as *f.* and *ff.* The term can also be used to denote a large volume size.

FORE EDGE

The edge of a book, opposite the SPINE. The fore edge sometimes carries painted decoration or images (fore-edge painting) or labeling for shelving purposes.

FRAME RULING

RULING that provides a frame to contain the text block. See also MISE-EN-PAGE.

FRETWORK

Ornament featuring a repeated, openwork rectilinear geometric pattern.

FULLY PAINTED

A fully painted ILLUMINATION is one that has been rendered throughout in PIGMENTS rather than wholly or partly in tint or line alone (see OUTLINE DRAWING and TINTED DRAWING).

GALLNUT

A swelling that forms on the bark of an oak tree after it has been stung by an insect laying its eggs. Tannic and gallic acids contained in gallnuts can be soaked out in water, the gall solution forming the basis of INK. Gall can also be used in tanning processes.

GATHERING

See QUIRE.

GAUFFERED

Gauffered pages have tooling (see TOOLED) on their opening edges.

GERMANIC

The Germanic peoples originated in the Iron Age. Beginning in the late fourth century, they increasingly settled, or conquered, what had been the western Roman Empire, forming a number of successor states (such as Frankia, ANGLO-SAXON England, Visigothic Spain, and Ostrogothic and Lombardic Italy). Although initially largely illiterate, they brought with them a vigorous art style, characterized by zoomorphic ornament and INTERLACE patterns. They made a major contribution to the development of INSULAR and PRE-CAROLINGIAN art and book production, and fostered regional developments in SCRIPT and language.

GESSO

A thick, water-base paint commonly formed of plaster, CHALK, or gypsum bound together with a glue. Gesso is used in manuscript ILLUMINATION as a GROUND for some GILDING processes, since it forms a raised surface ideal for BURNISHING and tooling (see TOOLED). Methods of gesso preparation varied.

GILDING

The application of gold or silver to a surface. Gold could be applied as an INK, in an expensive powdered form, for use in detailed work and in CHRYSOGRAPHY, but it was more frequently applied in medieval ILLUMINATION in the form of gold leaf. The gold leaf could simply be laid down on an area to which a BINDING MEDIUM such as glair or gum (perhaps mixed with honey to prevent it from cracking) had been applied, as was the case during the early Middle Ages; it could also be laid on a raised GROUND of

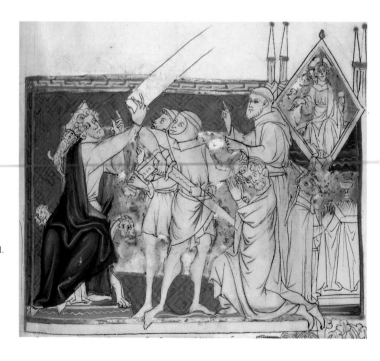

GILDING

Persecution by the Antichrist.
Abingdon Apocalypse.
England (London?), c.
1270–75. 33×21.5 cm
(13×8⁷⁄₁₆ in.). BL, Add.
Ms. 42555, fol. 41 (detail).

In this unfinished miniature, the gilding has been done but the colors were never fully completed.

GESSO. In order to enrich the tonality of the gold and to make the areas to which the ground had been applied more visible, a colorant such as bole (a pink earth color) was often added to the base. Gesso grounds enabled the gilded surface to be TOOLED. However it was applied, the gold could be BURNISHED or left in its slightly duller state. Gilding formed the first stage in the painting processes of illumination, since it was a messy activity, the gilded area often requiring trimming with a KNIFE. The gilding of a manuscript illustration was carried out by the artist or by a specialist.

GIRDLE BOOK

A small portable book attached to a girdle or belt. Girdle books were most often BOOKS OF HOURS or PRAYER BOOKS carried for devotional purposes (especially by wealthy women) and frequently had high-quality metalwork BINDINGS. They were particularly popular during the fifteenth and sixteenth centuries. Notebooks and sets of small wax TABLETS were also worn on the belt. See also VADE MECUM.

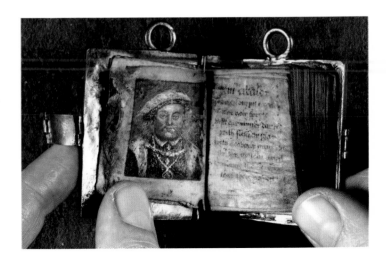

GIRDLE BOOK
King Henry VIII of England.
John Croke, Psalms in
English verse. England
(London), c. 1540. Leaf:
4.8 × 3.5 cm (1⅞ × 1⅜ in.).
BL, Stowe Ms. 956, fols.
1v–2.

GLAIR

See BINDING MEDIUM.

GLOSS

A word or words commenting on, elucidating, or translating those of the main text. Glosses were often written in the margins or between the lines. See also MISE-EN-PAGE and the illustration accompanying BIBLE.

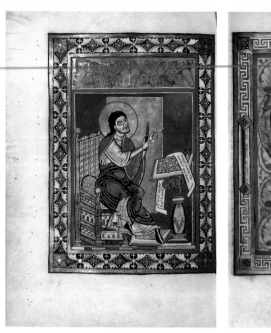
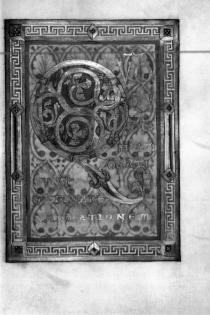

GOSPEL BOOK

Saint Luke; framed incipit page. Helmarshausen Gospels. Germany (Helmarshausen), 1120–40.
Leaf: 22.8 × 16.4 cm (9 × 6⁷⁄₁₆ in.). JPGM, Ms. Ludwig II 3 (83.MB.67), fols. 83v–84.

GOSPEL BOOK

The full text of the Gospels (the four accounts of Christ's life attributed to Matthew, Mark, Luke, and John, respectively), often accompanied by introductory matter such as the *Prefaces* of Saint Jerome, Eusebius' CANON TABLES (with or without corresponding marginal numbers in the text indicating Eusebian sections or chapter numbers), and chapter lists (*capitula*). By the seventh century, what had been a practice of continuous reading from the Gospels during daily Church services (*lectio continua*), with specific passages prescribed only for major feasts, was replaced by the assignment of a specific passage (pericope) for each day. Gospel lists (capitularies), which listed pericopes by their INCIPITS and EXPLICITS and were arranged to follow the liturgical year, were often included in Gospel books.

CARPET PAGES, INCIPIT PAGES, CHI-RHO pages, EVANGELIST PORTRAITS or SYMBOLS, and other illustrations appeared in Gospel books from the seventh century on. There are a number of sumptuous early medieval Gospel books (many of them connected with important cults and PATRONS), as well as working versions used in the LITURGY and Irish pocket Gospels. From the late eighth century, Gospel books were partially replaced in liturgical use by EVANGELARIES, containing the Gospel readings for the year. See the illustrations accompanying BYZANTINE, CANON TABLES, EARLY CHRISTIAN, and INSULAR.

GOSPEL LECTIONARY   See EVANGELARY.

GOTHIC

A term coined by the art critic Giorgio Vasari in the sixteenth century to describe what he considered to be the barbaric art of the West, that is, the art produced between ANTIQUITY and the RENAISSANCE. It is now used to describe a period of Western art that began in the late twelfth century and ended sometime between c. 1300 and the early sixteenth century, depending on the region in question and the rapidity of its response to the Renaissance. There were chronological and regional stylistic differences during this period, but the underlying, international characteristics of Gothic art included: a love of the courtly and of the GROTESQUE, which might coexist; an interest in an essentially NATURALISTIC depiction of the figure (although a penchant for courtly elegance, along with MANNERED or EXPRESSIONISTIC styles could intrude); and a decorative approach to INITIALS, frames, and backgrounds, with greater use of GILDING (during the later Middle Ages, this tendency gave way to a growing interest in landscape and perspective). In the Gothic period, the range of books produced became increasingly diversified (varying from biblical volumes and BOOKS OF HOURS to SCHOOL BOOKS, ROMANCES, and almanacs). Moreover, SECULAR PRODUCTION and consumption increased, with cities emerging alongside and then surpassing monasteries as important production centers.

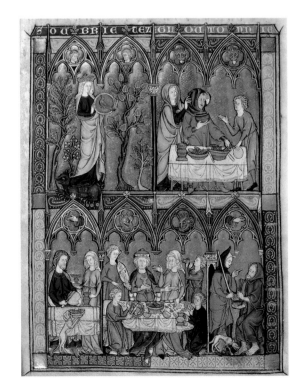

GOTHIC
Sobriety; Gluttony; A Frugal Meal; Dives and Lazarus. Frère Laurent, *La Somme le roi.* France (Lorraine), before 1294. 26 × 18 cm (10¼ × 7¹⁄₁₆ in.). BL, Add. Ms. 28162, fol. 10v.

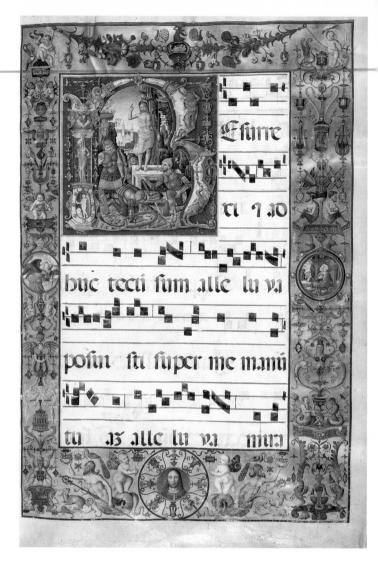

GRADUAL

Antonio da Monza. Initial *R* with *The Resurrection*. Gradual. Italy (Rome), late 15th or early 16th century. 63.5×43.5 cm (25×17⅛ in.). JPGM, Ms. Ludwig VI 3 (83.MH.86), fol. 16.

GRADUAL

A gradual is the response and versicle to the Epistle reading that constitutes one part of the MASS. The name derives from the practice of singing the gradual on the steps of the raised pulpit. More commonly, however, the term refers to the principal CHOIR BOOK used in the mass. Arranged according to the liturgical year (with TEMPORALE, SANCTORALE, and Common of Saints), a gradual contains (in addition to the graduals themselves) introits, tracts, alleluias, offertories, and communions. The introits—the first sung elements of the mass—were often introduced by HISTORIATED INITIALS (*Ad te levavi*, the introit for the first Sunday in Advent, being the most elaborate). For low mass, the contents of the gradual were included in the MISSAL and performed by the celebrant rather than the choir.

GRISAILLE

Monochrome painting, generally employing shades of gray (the term derives from *gris*, the French word for "gray"), executed in a black PIGMENT (such as a carbon-based lampblack) and an inert white pigment. Grisaille first appeared in the late thirteenth century but was especially popular from the second half of the fourteenth through the fifteenth century. Semi-grisaille, with landscape and flesh areas executed in color, characterized ILLUMINATION at the court of King Charles V of France (r. 1364–80). *Camaïeu* is a related technique that employs colors other than gray to create a monochrome painting or decorative component.

GROTESQUE

A hybrid and comic figure, often combining elements from various human and animal forms. Grotesques often bear no obvious relationship to the texts they embellish, although they can carry a commonly understood meaning derived, for example, from BESTIARY-related texts. They were popular in GOTHIC art from the thirteenth century on, especially as MARGINALIA. See also DROLLERY. See illustration on next page.

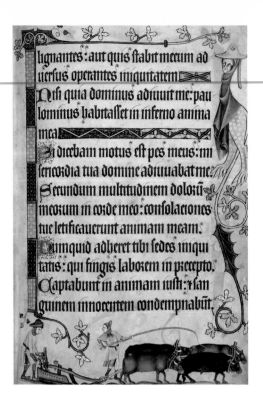

GROTESQUE
Plowing Scene and marginal grotesque. Luttrell Psalter. England (Diocese of Lincoln), c. 1325–35. 35×24.5 cm (13¾×9⅝ in.). BL, Add. Ms. 42130, fol. 170.

GROUND

The writing or painting surface, which may already have been covered with a layer of paint, or the base for metallic PIGMENT such as GESSO or gum. See also BINDING MEDIUM and GILDING.

GUARD

A protective support at the sewing edge of a manuscript. During the Middle Ages, PARCHMENT guards were sometimes folded around the spinal edge of a QUIRE or BIFOLIUM to strengthen it, especially in early PAPER manuscripts. In the process of modern rebinding, leaves are often mounted on guards to protect them and to reveal the maximum amount of codicological information.

GUIDE LETTER

A letter written (often by the SCRIBE) to tell the ILLUMINATOR which INITIAL or LITTERA NOTABILIOR to supply. Indications concerning which color was to be used (color notes) and fuller notes relating to the subject matter of an image might also be given, often in HARD POINT or METAL POINT to render them less obtrusive.

GUTTER

The place where BIFOLIA of writing material are folded and meet the SPINE inside a CODEX.

GYMNASTIC INITIAL

An INITIAL composed of lively, acrobatic human and/or animal figures. Gymnastic initials are particularly characteristic of ROMANESQUE illumination. Gymnastic decoration can occur in other contexts as well.

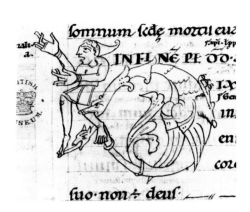

HAGIOGRAPHY

See SAINTS' LIVES.

HAIR SIDE

The side of a sheet of PARCHMENT or vellum that once carried the animal's hair. This side is generally darker and smoother than the FLESH SIDE and may carry speckled traces of hair follicles.

HALF SHEET

See SINGLETON.

HARD POINT

A pointed implement of metal or bone (often a STYLUS) used for RULING, drawing, and annotation. A hard point leaves a ridge-and-furrow effect on the writing surface rather than a graphic mark. See also INSTRUCTIONS, LEAD POINT, and METAL POINT.

HEAD

The top edge of a manuscript.

HEADBAND

See ENDBANDS.

HEADPIECE

A panel of ornament, sometimes incorporating a rubric or heading, that stands at the beginning of a text. The use of headpieces was inherited by the medieval West from LATE ANTIQUE and BYZANTINE book production and enjoyed particular popularity during the RENAISSANCE.

HERALDRY

The science of describing armorial bearings. Heraldry developed in the West during the twelfth century and evolved along with concepts of nobility and chivalry during the thirteenth and fourteenth centuries. Military identification symbols had been known in ANTIQUITY, but their systematic use emerged as an adjunct to medieval feudalism, serving to identify knights in full armor. Heraldic DEVICES were employed by secular society, by the Church, and by guilds and corporations. By the fourteenth century, strict rules concerning the significance of different components of a coat of arms were in full force.

The language of heraldry is French. There is an elaborate vocabulary for the blazoning (or describing) of a shield, involving its tinctures (color), charges (geometric patterns, called ordinaries, or the figures or objects depicted), and the way in which the arms are "differenced" to indicate collateral branches. Helmets and supporters (figures such as the lion and the unicorn, supporting the shield) also obey complex rules and nomenclatures. Many illuminated genealogies, pedigrees, and heraldic manuals were produced during the later Middle Ages. The occurrence of heraldic devices within manuscripts also yields valuable evidence concerning ownership. See also EMBLEM and MOTTO.

HERBAL

A text dealing with plants and their properties, often medicinal. Medieval herbals were frequently illustrated.

The study of plants formed part of natural philosophy during

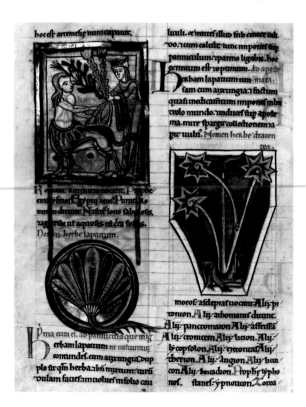

HERBAL
Artemis Giving the Herb Artemisia Leptasillos to a Centaur, The Herb Lepatium, and The Herb Dracontea. De medicina botanica. Northern England, c. 1190–1200. 29.5 × 20 cm (11⅝ × 7⅞ in.). BL, Sloane Ms. 1975, fol. 17v.

ANTIQUITY. Among the major authors of botanical texts written from the fourth century B.C. to the fourth century A.D. are Aristotle, Theophrastus (*Historia plantarum*), Hippocrates, Crateuas, Pliny the Elder (*Historia naturalis*), Dioscorides (*De materia medica*), and Pseudo-Apuleius Platonicus (*Herbarium*). Several of these works were probably illustrated during Antiquity. Southern Italy (especially centers such as Squillace, Monte Cassino, and Salerno) preserved the classical interest in botany and its medicinal application into the Middle Ages. The CAROLINGIAN and ANGLO-SAXON worlds did much to perpetuate interest in several botanical texts (notably the works of Dioscorides and Pseudo-Apuleius), England producing the first VERNACULAR translation of the *Herbarium*, perhaps as early as 1000. These early medieval copies contain cycles of illustrations which seem to represent for the most part copies of Antique cycles. It is clear from the errors in these depictions that the illuminators had no direct knowledge of some of the plants, and they retained images of classical deities such as Diana, Asclepius (god of medicine), and Mercury as well as the centaur Chiron, legendary teacher of Asclepius.

Illuminated herbals continued to be produced throughout the Middle Ages primarily as LIBRARY BOOKS, and their illustrations became progressively more STYLIZED. The Islamic world, however, had also preserved—and expanded—knowledge of classical botany, which from the late eleventh century on was transmitted to the West. At the medical school of Salerno in the mid-twelfth century, the *Circa instans*, containing remedies, or simples, from Latin and Arabic sources, was compiled. Some manuscripts of the *Circa instans* (also known as the *Liber simplici medicina* or *Secreta salernitana*) and the slightly later *Tacuinum sanitatis*, from northern Italy, have illustrations of plants based on the direct observation of nature rather than on images in earlier herbals. This more scientific trend was perpetuated in works such as the *Herbolario volgare* (*Popular Herbal*), an Italian translation by Jacopo Filippo of an Arabic treatise by Serapion the Younger, and initiated the RENAISSANCE tradition of naturalistically illustrated herbals. See also CLASSICAL TEXTS and MEDICAL TEXTS.

HEXATEUCH

The first six books of the Old Testament, which were sometimes contained in a single, separate volume.

HIBERNO-SAXON

See INSULAR.

HIERARCHY

A system for arranging elements in a series according to formal or functional degrees of importance. A hierarchy can be applied to decorative elements, which may vary in content to include MINIATURES, TITLE PIECES, HEADPIECES, TAILPIECES, BORDERS, major

INITIALS, minor initials, LITTERAE FLORISSAE, LITTERAE NOTABI-
LIORES, LINE FILLERS, RUN-OVER SYMBOLS, BAS-DE-PAGE scenes,
and MARGINALIA. Each illuminated manuscript displays its own
hierarchy of decoration, whose various elements may contain a
number of grades to indicate the relative importance of a section
of text or to highlight and differentiate textual divisions.

HISTORIATED INITIAL

A letter containing an identifiable scene or figures, sometimes
relating to the text. Historiated initials, first encountered in INSU-
LAR illumination of the first half of the eighth century, became a
popular feature of medieval ILLUMINATION. BORDERS can also be
historiated.

HISTORIATED INITIAL
Initial *I* with *Seven Scenes
from the Creation* and *The
Crucifixion*. Bible. France
(probably Lille), c. 1270.
47×32.2 cm (18½×12¹¹⁄₁₆
in.). JPGM, Ms. Ludwig I 8
(83.MA.57), vol. 1, fol. 10v.

HISTORY TEXTS   See CHRONICLE.

HOMILIARY

A book containing homilies (discussions of biblical passages, usually from the Gospels), arranged according to the ecclesiastical year. It is also known as a *sermologus*.

HORAE

See BOOK OF HOURS.

HUMANISTIC

Humanism, an important component of the RENAISSANCE, is a system of study characterized by a revival of classical learning that originated in Florence in the late fourteenth century. As an adjunct to this revival, the conscious reformation of SCRIPT and book design was promoted during the fourteenth and fifteenth centuries by Italian humanists such as Petrarch, Poggio Bracciolini, Niccolò Niccoli, and Coluccio Salutati. Florence and Rome were at the forefront of humanistic book production, with other centers such as Milan and Bologna remaining more conservative. Nonetheless, the force of the movement was felt throughout Europe from the later fifteenth century on. See the illustrations accompanying RENAISSANCE and WHITE VINE-STEM.

HYMNAL

A book, also called a hymnary, containing metrical hymns sung in the DIVINE OFFICE and arranged according to the liturgical year. The hymnal could be included in a PSALTER or ANTIPHONAL as a separate section. Its contents were eventually incorporated into the BREVIARY.

ICON

An icon (the Greek word for "image") is a likeness of a sacred personage or subject that is venerated. Icons originated in the BYZANTINE Church, typically in the form of small paintings on wood supports, but their influence can be perceived in Western art.

ICONOGRAPHY

In general terms, the subject of a picture is called its iconography. More specifically, iconography is the study of the meaning of images, including their symbolic content. The eagle, for example, may be interpreted as a symbol of Christ (from its interpretation in the BESTIARY and related texts) or of the evangelist Saint John (see EVANGELIST SYMBOLS) and is linked in exegesis with the Resurrection.

ILLUMINATION

Illumination, from the Latin *illuminare*, "to enlighten or illuminate," is the embellishment of a manuscript with luminous colors (especially gold and silver). In the past, the coloring of maps and prints was also called illumination. A MINIATURE is sometimes referred to as an illumination.

An artist producing ILLUMINATION. The illuminator could, on occasion, also be the SCRIBE. During late ANTIQUITY, illuminators constituted a professional class. In the early Middle Ages, they worked within an ecclesiastical SCRIPTORIUM as part of a team or were attached to a court. It has been suggested that there were even some itinerant illuminators. Following the rise of the universities around 1200, illuminators were generally based in urban centers (although many monastic scriptoria, with resident or outside illuminators, continued to function). In the cities, illuminators often lived in the same neighborhood and frequently collaborated (see WORKSHOP and SCHOOL OF ILLUMINATION).

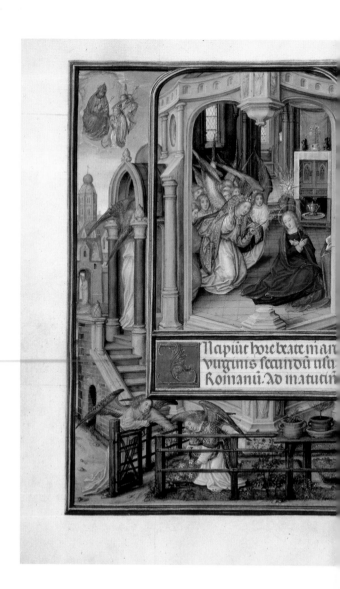

Illuminators could be male or female and members of monastic or minor clerical orders; from about 1200 members of the laity increasingly took up the profession. By the late Middle Ages, most illuminators were LAY people. Illuminators continued to practice their art, although to a limited extent, after the introduction of printing, sometimes embellishing early printed books, and often working in the field of professional CALLIGRAPHY.

ILLUSIONISTIC

Illusionistic painting is that which successfully creates the impression of three-dimensional space on a two-dimensional surface.

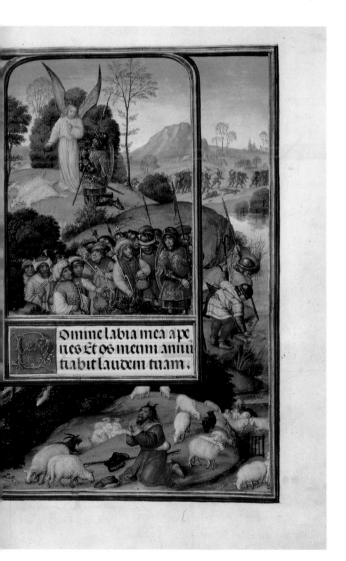

These pages show a sophisticated play of illusionism. In the page on the right, for example, miniature and border zones (which contain scenes separate in time and space) are divided by a frame, but the landscape and Gideon's army appear to continue behind the frame, linking the two zones.

IMPRESSIONISTIC

Impressionistic painting conveys the appearance of natural things by suggesting light, movement, and space without rendering them in a precise, veristic fashion. See the illustration accompanying LATE ANTIQUE.

INCIPIT

The opening words of a text, from the Latin verb *incipere* ("to begin"). The incipit and EXPLICIT of a book or text are often used in place of a title to identify a text.

INCIPIT PAGE

The opening of a major section of text that is embellished with a large INITIAL or monogram and DISPLAY SCRIPT. See the illustration accompanying INSULAR.

INCUNABLE

From the Latin *in cunabula* ("in the cradle" or "origins"), an incunable is a printed book produced before 1501, that is, when the process of printing from movable type was in its infancy. See also XYLOGRAPH.

INHABITED INITIAL

An enlarged letter at the beginning of a chapter, paragraph, or important section of a text that contains human or animal figures but not an identifiable narrative scene (which is a HISTORIATED INITIAL). Inhabited initials are particularly characteristic of ROMANESQUE illumination. BORDERS can also be inhabited.

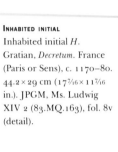

INHABITED INITIAL
Inhabited initial *H*.
Gratian, *Decretum*. France
(Paris or Sens), c. 1170–80.
44.2 × 29 cm (17⁷⁄₁₆ × 11⁷⁄₁₆
in.). JPGM, Ms. Ludwig
XIV 2 (83.MQ.163), fol. 8v
(detail).

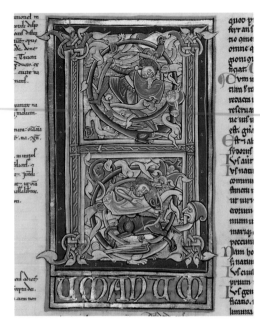

INITIAL

An enlarged and decorated letter introducing an important section of a text. Initials can have different levels of significance, according to the divisions of the text or their place within a program of decoration (see HIERARCHY). Among these levels are major initials, minor initials (sometimes in several grades), LITTERAE FLORISSAE, and more frequent minor textual breaks; these latter are marked by LITTERAE NOTABILIORES, which serve as an adjunct to punctuation. Major and minor initials can be painted or rendered in PEN (see PENWORK INITIAL). Among the most common forms of initials are DECORATED, ANTHROPOMORPHIC, ZOOMORPHIC, ZOO-ANTHROPOMORPHIC, GYMNASTIC, INHABITED, or HISTORIATED.

INK

The word derives from the Latin *encaustum* ("burnt in"), since the gallic and tannic acids in ink and the oxidation of its ingredients cause it to eat into the writing surface. The basis of medieval ink was a solution of gall (from GALLNUTS) and gum, colored by the addition of carbon (lampblack) and/or iron salts. The ferrous ink produced by iron salts sometimes faded to a red-brown or yellow. Copper salts were occasionally used too, sometimes fading to gray-green. Ink was used for drawing and RULING as well as for writing and, when diluted, could be applied with a BRUSH as a wash.

INSTRUCTIONS

STATIONERS, SCRIBES, or ILLUMINATORS often gave written instructions as to the form, content, or color of what was to be painted. Instructions relating to BINDING and assembly also occur. Such instructions were often executed in HARD POINT, LEAD POINT, or METAL POINT in order to render them less intrusive.

INSTRUCTIONS

The Betrayal of Christ.
Rudolf von Ems,
Weltchronik and other texts.
Germany (Bavaria),
c. 1405–10. 33.5 × 23.5 cm
(13³⁄₁₆ × 9¼ in.). JPGM, Ms.
33 (88.MP.70), fol. 288
(detail).

The note in the bottom margin provides the illuminator with instructions concerning the subject of the miniature.

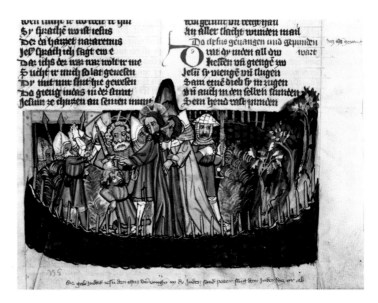

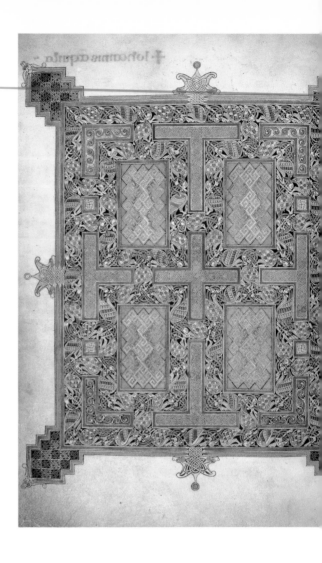

Insular refers to a period of close cultural interaction between Britain and Ireland, from around 550 to 900. Elements of CELTIC, GERMANIC, antique, EARLY CHRISTIAN, and Mediterranean culture fused together to form something new, entirely the product of the islands of Britain and Ireland. Insular art and learning in turn stimulated cultural development on the Continent (including the CAROLINGIAN renaissance) and played a significant role in the evolution of ROMANESQUE art.

A characteristic feature of Insular book production is the integration of decoration, SCRIPT, and text. The earliest developments in Insular manuscript art seem to have occurred in sixth-seventh century Ireland and its outposts. Examples include the Cathach of Saint Columba and the products of the Irish monastic foundation of Bobbio in northern Italy. Irish influence was transmitted to

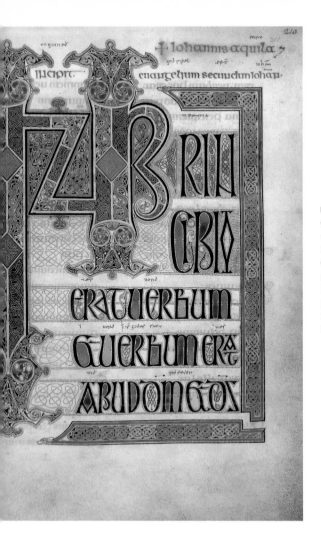

INSULAR
Carpet page; incipit page
with decorated *INP*
ligature. Lindisfarne
Gospels. England
(Northumbria,
Lindisfarne), c. 700. Leaf:
34 × 24.5 cm (13⅜ × 9⅝ in.).
BL, Cotton Ms. Nero D.IV,
fols. 210v–211.

England and Scotland, where it fused with Germanic and Pictish
artistic styles, producing a spectacular hybrid form known as
Hiberno-Saxon art, which includes such monuments as the Book
of Durrow, the Lindisfarne Gospels, and the Book of Kells. The
influence of Rome and the Mediterranean is also found in these
works, but it made a more overt visual mark on the products of
SCRIPTORIA of romanizing monastic foundations, such as those at
Canterbury and Monkwearmouth/Jarrow (seen in the Vespasian
PSALTER and the CODEX Amiatinus). Echoes of Hiberno-Saxon art,
combined with the romanizing tradition and with influences from
PRE-CAROLINGIAN and Carolingian Gaul, gave rise to an important
group of southern English manuscripts, the so-called Tiberius
Group or Canterbury Group. Insular influence was also felt in
later ANGLO-SAXON manuscript production.

INTERLACE   Decoration consisting of apparently interwoven straps or ribbons. Interlace was known in ANTIQUITY and much favored in GERMANIC art, whence it was transmitted to INSULAR art, which further developed the form. Interlace also survived in parts of Italy and in COPTIC Egypt. See the illustration accompanying INSULAR.

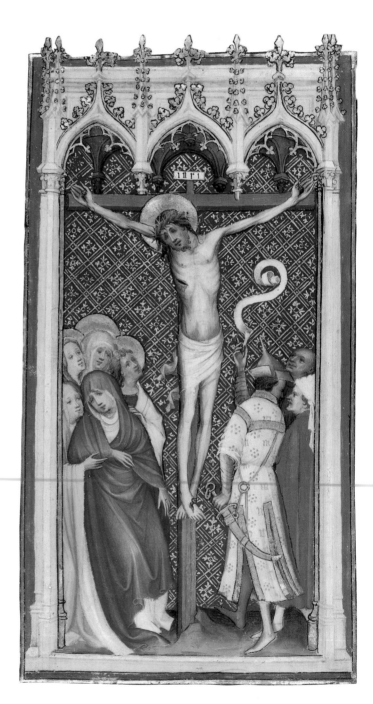

INTERNATIONAL STYLE
Master of Saint Veronica. *Crucifixion.* Cutting from a manuscript. Germany (Cologne), c. 1400–10. 23.6 × 12 cm (9⁵⁄₁₆ × 4¾ in.). JPGM, Ms. Ludwig Folia 2 (83.MS.49), leaf 1.

INTERNATIONAL STYLE   A term coined at the end of the nineteenth century to denote a style of late GOTHIC art, practiced in the late fourteenth and early fifteenth centuries. The International Style fused diverse artistic traditions (primarily those of Paris, Holland, and Bohemia) which, owing to the complex interrelationships of its courtly PATRONS, assumed an international diffusion throughout Europe. Courtly patronage, an elegant and refined rendering of forms, and generally sumptuous quality distinguish these works. Important artists include the Limbourg brothers, the MASTER of the Brussels Initials, Jacquemart de Hesdin, the Bedford Master, the Boucicaut Master, John Siferwas, Herman Scheere, Giovannino de' Grassi, and Belbello da Pavia. Among the most significant patrons were King Wenceslaus IV of Bohemia; King Martin of Aragon; King Charles VI of France; Jean, Duke of Berry; King Richard II of England; John, Duke of Bedford, and his wife, Anne of Burgundy; Philip the Bold, Duke of Burgundy (see BURGUNDIAN); and Gian Galeazzo Visconti, Duke of Milan.

JOURNAL   See DIURNAL.

KETTLE STITCH   A stitch at or near the HEAD and TAIL of a manuscript that links a QUIRE to the preceding one during sewing.

KNIFE   A pen knife was used by SCRIBES for a number of purposes, including PRICKING, cutting the nib of a quill PEN, and CORRECTION by scraping out errors. Medieval depictions of SCRIBES often show them holding a quill in one hand and a knife in the other. The counterbalance of tools was not only convenient, but it helped to achieve an even pressure of SCRIPT and to secure the writing surface.

KYRIALE   The portion of a GRADUAL containing the ordinary chants (*Kyrie, Gloria, Credo, Sanctus,* and *Agnus dei*) of the MASS, that is, the chants whose texts remain unchanged throughout the ecclesiastical year. In the late Middle Ages, the kyriale sometimes formed a separate volume.

LABORS OF THE MONTHS   See OCCUPATIONAL CALENDAR.

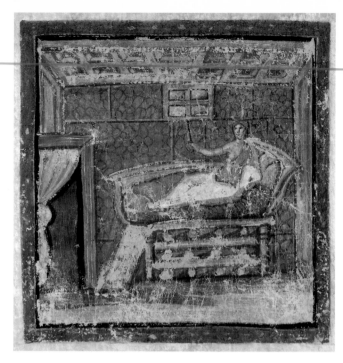

The Death of Dido. Vergil, *Aeneis* and *Georgica*. Italy (Rome), early 5th century. 21.9 × 19.6 cm (8⅝ × 7¹¹⁄₁₆ in.).
Biblioteca Apostolica Vaticana (Vatican City), Ms. Vat. lat. 3225, fol. 40.

LATE ANTIQUE

Late ANTIQUITY is the period from the reign of Emperor Constantine the Great (306–37) to the disintegration of the western Roman Empire in the fifth century and the rise of a strong eastern Empire during the reign of Justinian (527–65).

LAY

A lay person is one who belongs to secular society, that is, who is neither a cleric nor a member of a religious order.

LEAD POINT

A lead point, also known as *plummet*, is a piece of lead alloy, sometimes contained in a holder (the precursor of the pencil), which could be used for drawing, annotation, and RULING. Lead point began to be widely used in the eleventh and twelfth centuries. Graphite, derived from carbon, was not generally used before the seventeenth century. See also HARD POINT and METAL POINT.

LEAF

See FOLIO.

LECTIONARY

A volume containing readings for use in the LITURGY. See also DIVINE OFFICE, EPISTOLARY, EVANGELARY, and MASS.

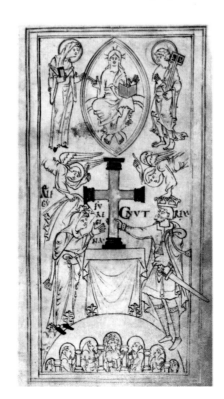

vem: habit uitam etemam. Et ego
resuscitabo eum: in nouissimo die

LECTIONARY

Lord Lovell Receiving a Lectionary from the Dominican Illuminator John Siferwas. Lovell Lectionary. Southwestern England, late 14th century. 47×33 cm (18½×13 in.). BL, Harley Ms. 7026, fol. 4v.

LIBER VITAE

A book listing the *familiares* ("members") and benefactors of a monastic community who were to be remembered in its MASSES and in other services and prayers. It was usually read with the

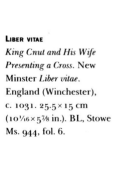

LIBER VITAE

King Cnut and His Wife Presenting a Cross. New Minster *Liber vitae.* England (Winchester), c. 1031. 25.5×15 cm (10 1/16×5 7/8 in.). BL, Stowe Ms. 944, fol. 6.

MARTYROLOGY and the obituary at the canonical hour of prime. Those listed were sometimes depicted in the manuscript.

LIBRAIRE	See STATIONER.

LIBRARY BOOK   The medieval monastic library contained a wide variety of texts, from biblical and liturgical volumes (the more important and/or luxurious of these often being housed in the sacristy or elsewhere in the church), PATRISTIC works, COMMENTARIES, CHRONICLES, SCHOOL BOOKS, legal tomes (such as DIGESTS and DECRETALS), selected CLASSICAL TEXTS, MEDICAL TEXTS, HERBALS, and certain ASTRONOMICAL/ASTROLOGICAL TEXTS. Secular institutions, such as colleges, also had libraries. Some secular scholars—especially the humanists (see HUMANISTIC)—had personal collections of books, as did bibliophiles, who were often aristocrats. The contents of secular libraries varied according to their owners' interests.

The methods of marking books for storage and of cataloguing or listing them often provide valuable PROVENANCE information. Before the introduction of upright storage shelves in the fifteenth century, books were generally stored flat in a closet known as an *armarium*, in a chest, or on a circular lectern called a *rota*, or were chained to a lectern (see CHAINED BOOK). Many library books were quite modest, inexpensive products, while others (such as biblical and liturgical volumes, chronicles, and ROMANCES) were often richly illuminated.

LIMP BINDING   A BINDING composed of PARCHMENT, PAPER, or fabric, without BOARDS. Limp bindings were generally used during the later Middle Ages and early modern period for less expensive books.

LINE FILLER   A decorative device (abstract, foliate, zoomorphic, or anthropomorphic) that fills the remainder of a line not fully occupied by SCRIPT. Line fillers were initially popularized in INSULAR and PRE-CAROLINGIAN art.

LITANY OF THE SAINTS   The litany is a series of invocations for deliverance and intercession usually addressed to the Trinity, the Virgin, angels, apostles, martyrs, confessors, and virgins, individually and as groups. Such litanies are encountered in the East from the third century and the West from the late fifth century. The saints included in a litany varied according to region and patronage. For this reason, they often yield valuable evidence concerning the ORIGIN of a manuscript. Litanies of saints increased in length throughout the Middle Ages. See also SUFFRAGE.

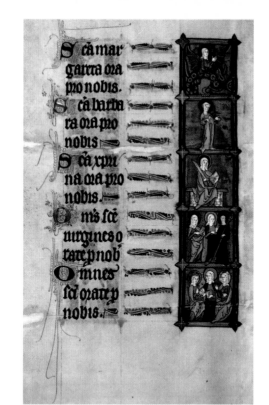

LITANY OF THE SAINTS
Saints Margaret, Barbara, and Christina, and the Holy Virgins. Ruskin Hours. Northern France, early 14th century. 26.4 × 18.4 cm (10⅜ × 7¼ in.). JPGM, Ms. Ludwig IX 3 (83.ML.99), fol. 106v.

LITTERA FLORISSA
(pl. LITTERAE FLORISSAE)

A PEN-FLOURISHED letter or INITIAL, usually composed of delicate geometric and foliate motifs.

LITTERA NOTABILIOR
(pl. LITTERAE
NOTABILIORES)

An enlarged letter within a text, designed to clarify the syntax of a passage.

LITURGY

Rites, observances, or procedures prescribed for public worship. At the core of Christian liturgy are the MASS (the celebration of the Eucharist) and the DIVINE OFFICE.

MANNERED

A mannered style is one that appears self-conscious and somewhat artificial. See the illustration accompanying EXPRESSIONISTIC.

MANUSCRIPT

The word manuscript, literally "handwritten," has come to be used to describe a book written by hand. It is abbreviated as *ms.* (singular) and *mss.* (plural).

MAPPA MUNDI

(pl. MAPPAE MUNDI)

A world map. Mappae mundi are known to have been produced during ANTIQUITY, but the earliest surviving example is in an ANGLO-SAXON book of the early eleventh century. During the GOTHIC period, illuminated mappae mundi were produced for inclusion in books and as altarpieces (such as the Hereford Mappa Mundi). They functioned as visual encyclopedias of world knowledge, incorporating material from biblical history and texts such as the *Marvels of the East* (concerning the mythical inhabitants of the East). In the later Middle Ages, thanks to developments in navigation and chart making, more detailed coastlines were grafted on to mappae mundi. Diagrammatic world maps, such as the *T maps* of Isidore of Seville, which depicted the three known continents as a T contained in a circle, were also produced during the Middle Ages.

MAPPA MUNDI

Mappa mundi with Christ and Censing Angels. Psalter. England (London?), c. 1262–70. 17 × 12.5 cm (6¹¹⁄₁₆ × 4¹⁵⁄₁₆ in.). BL, Add. Ms. 28681, fol. 9.

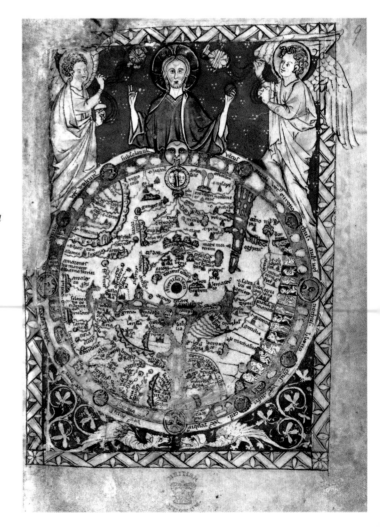

MARGINALIA

The Latin word for "things in the margin," marginalia refers to writing or decoration in the margins of a manuscript. Such features can form part of the original program of work, but they also can be of a secondary or even extraneous nature. Marginalia include GLOSSES, annotations, and diagrams. Fully developed BORDER decoration, especially that of the fifteenth century, is considered a separate genre or component of the decorative scheme. See the illustrations accompanying BIBLE and GROTESQUE.

MARTYROLOGY

A book, sometimes called a *passionale*, containing narrative readings on the lives and martyrdoms of the saints, to be read in the DIVINE OFFICE at the canonical hour of prime. The contents of a martyrology are arranged according to the SANCTORALE of the liturgical year.

MASS

Along with the DIVINE OFFICE, the mass forms the basis of Christian LITURGY. It centers on the Eucharist, the celebration of Christ's sacrifice, which derived from his actions at the Last Supper and the *agape*, or love feast, of the early Church. The term stems from the dismissal at the end of the celebration, *Ite, missa est* ("the dismissal is here"). The texts for the performance of the mass, which include practices and formulae added over the centuries, were first contained in the SACRAMENTARY and then in the MISSAL. The mass was attended daily by those in religious orders, the clergy, and, with varying frequency, by members of the laity.

MASTER

Frequently employed in names of convenience used to identify anonymous artists, the word also denotes an artist whose work is considered of importance and often of particularly high quality. Master ILLUMINATORS frequently attracted a following and employed others (perhaps to supply BORDERS, INITIALS, or minor decorative components, or to assist in painting MINIATURES and major decorative components). In some cases the name of the master is known (for example, the thirteenth-century Parisian illuminator Master Honoré), but the majority of masters are anonymous and are often identified by key examples of their work or by distinctive features of their style. Among fifteenth-century artists, the Master of Guillebert de Mets is named after a SCRIBE with whom he worked on a copy of Boccaccio's *Decameron*, and the Boucicaut Master is named after the Maréchal de Boucicaut, the PATRON of one of his most important manuscripts. The Masters of the Gold Scrolls are a group of Flemish artists so called because of their predilection for incorporating scroll work into their miniatures. See illustration on next page. See also SECULAR PRODUCTION.

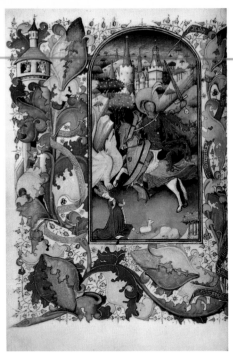
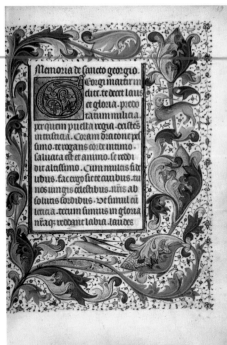

MASTER

Master of Guillebert de Mets. *Saint George Battling the Dragon*. Book of hours. Belgium (Tournai?), c. 1450–60.
Leaf: 19.4 × 14 cm (7⅝ × 5½ in.). JPGM, Ms. 2 (84.ML.67), fols. 18v–19.
The Master of Guillebert de Mets was responsible for the miniature of Saint George and the accompanying
historiated border on the page at the left. Comparison of the two pages reproduced here reveals that
the border on the right-hand page is a workshop product in the style of the master.

MEDICAL TEXTS

Texts concerning healing were frequently illustrated as an aid to
comprehension in ANTIQUITY, as evidenced by works such as the
Johnson PAPYRUS of c. 400 and the early HERBALS.

A number of ancient texts were preserved in the early medieval West, among them Dioscorides' *De materia medica*, the *Herbarium* of Pseudo-Apuleius Platonicus, and Placitus' *Liber medicinae ex
animalibus* (*On the Medicinal Qualities of Animals*). Other classical
treatises on medicine were preserved by Islamic scholars. Elements
of Christian charismatic healing and of Western pagan lore were
absorbed into this tradition, resulting in works such as the ANGLO-
SAXON leechbooks. Beginning in the late twelfth century, the natural philosophy of classical scholars such as Galen of Pergamon
exerted an influence. Galen's ideas and those of Hippocrates
were accompanied by the COMMENTARIES of Islamic scholars in
the *Articella*, a twelfth-century text. Islamic philosophical texts
containing medical data, such as those of Avicenna (eleventh
century) and Averroës (twelfth century), also influenced the West

during the thirteenth and fourteenth centuries. Practical treatises were composed in the high Middle Ages, including Roger Frugardi's *Chirurgia* (1180) and John Arderne's *Fistula in ano* (1376), along with manuals on health such as that by Aldobrandino da Siena of the thirteenth century.

Many of the illustrations accompanying medical works are diagrammatic, including depictions of the Zodiac Man, the Bloodletting Man, the Muscle Man, the Wound Man, and the Disease Woman, whose bodies are labeled with appropriate afflictions or symbols. The Zodiac Man, for example, shows the propitious time for treating various ailments in any part of the body. Luxuriously illuminated medical manuscripts were produced in the later Middle Ages, stimulated by the increase in secular patronage. Monastic libraries contained a number of medical manuscripts, and universities, notably those of Paris and Salerno, also contributed to the dissemination of these texts. See also CALENDAR, COMPUTUS TEXTS, and VADE MECUM.

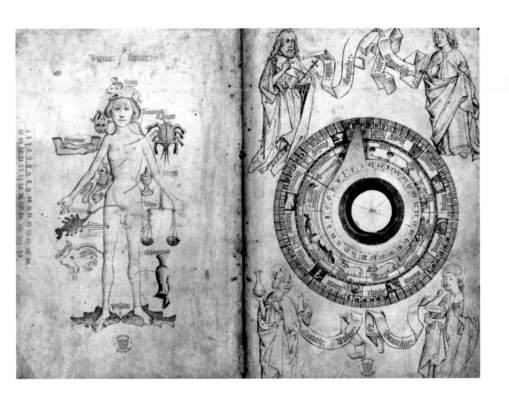

MEDICAL TEXTS

The Zodiac Man; a volvelle with saints. Guild Book of the Barber Surgeons of York. England (York), 15th century. Leaf: 34×23 cm (13⅜×9¹⁄₁₆ in.). BL, Egerton Ms. 2572, fols. 50v–51.

Membra disjecta	Detached leaves from a manuscript, the term is the Latin for "things scattered."
Memorial	~~See suffrage.~~
Metal point	A writing implement, made of metal and used for annotation, drawing, and RULING, which leaves a trace element on the writing surface. This mark varies in appearance according to the metal used (and any alloys present), with a ferrous point leaving a brown mark, silver and lead (LEAD POINT) leaving a silver-gray trace, and copper alloys sometimes leaving a gray-green mark. The marks produced are more discreet than those made with INK but more visible than those made with a HARD POINT. Metal point increased in use from the eleventh century on. INSTRUCTIONS to artists and BINDERS' notes were often executed in this medium.
Miniature	An independent illustration, as opposed to a scene incorporated into another element of the decorative scheme such as a BORDER or INITIAL. It takes its name from the Latin *miniare*, meaning "to color with red" (the adornment of books originally was executed in red, or *minium*).

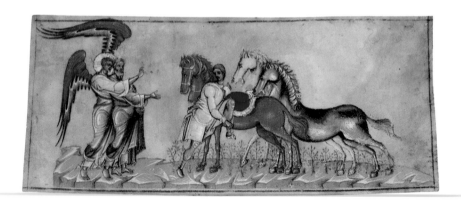

Miniature
Zachariah's Vision of the Man Mounting a Red Horse. Cutting from a manuscript of the Major and Minor Prophets. Italy (Sicily), late 13th century. 7.3 × 17.4 cm (2⅞ × 6⅞ in.). JPGM, Ms. 35 (88.MS.125), leaf 2.

Mise-en-page	This term refers to the layout of a page. Significant developments in the mise-en-page of manuscripts include the standardization of a one- or two-column layout during the LATE ANTIQUE and EARLY CHRISTIAN periods (initially four columns might be used, in emulation of an unrolled section of a ROLL). Experiments with complex layout and RULING patterns to accommodate GLOSSES, COMMENTARIES, and other parallel texts took place during the CAR-

OLINGIAN period and, notably, within university book production from the thirteenth century. Another important development was the standard adoption of a layout wherein the top line of text was written "below top-line" rather than "above top-line" of the ruling, a change that appeared around 1220–40 and which acts as a useful criterion for dating manuscripts.

MISSAL

A SERVICE BOOK containing the texts necessary for the performance of the MASS (including chants, prayers, and readings), together with ceremonial directions. The prayers and other texts recited by the priest were originally contained in the SACRAMENTARY, which was used together with the GRADUAL, the EVANGELARY, and the EPISTOLARY for the performance of high or solemn mass. The missal was introduced in the CAROLINGIAN period and by the thirteenth century had supplanted the older SACRAMENTARY, combining in one volume the various components for the performance of the mass. Its development was prompted by the custom of saying private masses and low masses, which were performed by the celebrant alone. Principal fields for decoration in the missal are the canon page (with the text *Te igitur*) and the *Vere dignum* monogram.

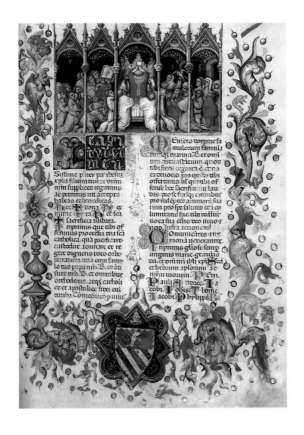

MISSAL

The Elevation of the Host.
Missal of the Anti-Pope
John XXIII. Italy
(Bologna), c. 1389–1406.
33 × 24 cm (13 × 9⁷⁄₁₆ in.).
JPGM, Ms. 34 (88.MG.71),
fol. 130.

MODEL

An image which inspires a copy or stimulates a response.

MODEL BOOK

A book in which artists recorded designs, of their own invention or copied from other sources, often accompanied by notes relating to color and composition. Many such books must have existed but very few have survived. Some late BYZANTINE examples are extant, and a famous Western medieval model book of the thirteenth century survives at Wolfenbüttel. Another important Western example is that produced by the artist Villard de Honnecourt, also in the thirteenth century. The early fifteenth-century sketchbook of Jacques D'Aliwe, executed on boxwood tablets, is a rare example of the sort of sketches that must have existed in quantity during the later Middle Ages. FLYLEAVES sometimes carry designs of the type found in model books. Waste materials such as fragments of wood, slate, or bone were often used to try out designs; these are known as *motif pieces*.

MODELED

Modeling is the technique of giving depicted objects the appearance of three-dimensionality through shading and highlighting. See the illustration accompanying PUTTO.

MONASTIC PRODUCTION

From the EARLY CHRISTIAN period until the rise of the universities around 1200, book production was largely centered in monastic SCRIPTORIA, with male and female religious participating in the work. A scriptorium could operate under a supervisor, and the work teams varied in composition, from a single artist-SCRIBE who was responsible for a whole book to extensive teams of scribes, ILLUMINATORS, correctors, and BINDERS. The sequence of work also varied, but the general procedure seems to have entailed the writing of the main text, its RUBRICATION, ILLUMINATION, and CORRECTION, followed by sewing and BINDING. Work in the scriptorium represented one part of the daily work in a monastic community, as prescribed by its rule. Monastic production continued alongside SECULAR PRODUCTION during the later Middle Ages.

MOTTO

A word or phrase attached to an EMBLEM, often explaining or emphasizing its symbolic value. In HERALDRY a motto is a word or phrase carried on a scroll and placed below an achievement of arms or above a crest. The motto can refer to the name or exploits of the bearer or to elements included in the arms or can simply be a pious expression.

MUSIC MANUSCRIPTS Manuscripts in which music appears, whether ecclesiastical or secular, were sometimes illuminated, the extent of ILLUMINATION depending largely on patronage and purpose. Depictions of musicians and instruments frequently appear in medieval manuscripts as DROLLERIES and in INITIALS and BAS-DE-PAGE scenes.

Music was incorporated into the Christian LITURGY early on, influenced by the use of music in the synagogue. The study of music theory was part of the Antique and medieval Liberal Arts syllabus. Plainchant (unison singing, originally unaccompanied) was the traditional music of the western Church. From about 1000, vocal polyphony (music with two or more melodically independent parts) was being practiced at Winchester in England. A particularly rich repertoire of polyphony came from the cathedral of Notre-Dame in Paris. Polyphony made certain chants of the MASS longer and more complex. From the mid-thirteenth century on, liturgical polyphony shared a number of characteristics with secular music.

There is little early written evidence for secular music, although there was probably a rich oral tradition, but collections of the songs of troubadours and trouvères survive from the mid-thirteenth century on, by which time the courtly poet-composer had achieved professional status.

The notation of liturgical music initially appears in the form of *neumes*—graphic symbols written above the text and indicating the rise and fall of melodic movement or repetitions of the same pitch. Twelve to fifteen regional families of neumes have been identified. They were commonly written on a four-line staff beginning in the mid-eleventh century. Two hundred years later, eastern European music manuscripts adopted *Gothic notation*, produced with a thick, square-cut nib, with the points and curves of earlier neumes being replaced by broader, more angular forms. A similar development in the Île de France gave rise to the use of *square notation* in the late twelfth century, especially in France and Italy. Alphabetical notation is also sporadically encountered from ANTIQUITY on in a theoretical context. For liturgical manuscripts with sung components, see ANTIPHONAL, BREVIARY, GRADUAL, HYMNAL, KYRIALE, MISSAL, SEQUENTIARY, and TROPER.

NATURALISTIC A naturalistic depiction in painting is one that seeks to represent the appearance of things, without artificiality or stylization.

NOCTURNAL See DIURNAL.

OBIT A note recording a death. Obits were often entered into liturgical CALENDARS to commemorate the deceased and can provide valuable PROVENANCE information.

OCCUPATIONAL CALENDAR A CALENDAR incorporating a series of illustrations, ultimately of classical origin, that depict the labors appropriate to each of the months (example, the labor for June is reaping, that for August, mowing). Images of the labors of the months began to appear in calendar decoration, along with zodiacal signs, in the ninth and tenth centuries and became increasingly elaborate and prominent during the later Middle Ages. The scenes were usually agrarian in character, but some fifteenth-century manuscripts (notably the Très Riches Heures of Jean de Berry and the Sforza Hours) juxtaposed these with scenes from courtly life.

OCTATEUCH The first eight books of the Old Testament.

OCTAVO A volume measuring one-eighth the size of a full sheet of writing material.

OFFICE See DIVINE OFFICE.

ORDINAL A guide to the celebration of the LITURGY, usually including instructions for liturgical actions to be carried out by the clergy.

ORIGIN The place of origin of a manuscript is seldom recorded (unless mentioned in a COLOPHON) and has to be assessed by a study of the book's contents, patronage, method of production, and PROVENANCE. The USE of a liturgical manuscript is not necessarily an indicator of its place of origin, since the major uses enjoyed a wide geographical currency.

ORTHOGRAPHY Certain orthographical, or spelling, variants may assist in localizing a manuscript. The INSULAR *ss*, for example, is a common variant of *s*. Orthographical practices can also help in the identification of SCRIBES.

OTTONIAN The Saxon Liudolfing, or Ottonian, dynasty ruled the East Frankish component of the CAROLINGIAN Empire from 919 to 1024. The dynasty's extensive patronage, along with that of its clerics and courtiers, encouraged the arts, contributing considerably to the transition from early medieval into ROMANESQUE. During this period art, religion, and politics were inextricably linked, with an emphasis on the interrelationship of Church and state and on the divine sanction of imperial rule. Stylistically, there was a noticeable continuity with Carolingian art, coupled with influences from

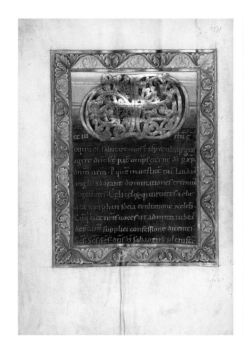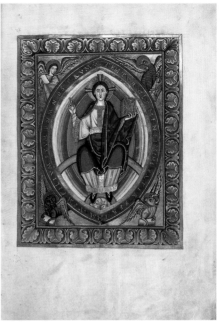

OTTONIAN

Framed incipit page; *Christ in Majesty*. Sacramentary. Germany (Mainz), second quarter of the 11th century. Leaf: 26.6 × 19.1 cm (10½ × 7⁹⁄₁₆ in.). JPGM, Ms. Ludwig V 2 (83.MF.77), fols. 21v–22.

Italy, ANGLO-SAXON England and, most important, from BYZANTINE art. The marriage of Otto II (955–983) to a Byzantine princess, Theophano, who would later act as regent for her son, the future Otto III (980–1002), played a significant role in transmitting Byzantine influences to the West. Many of the books of this period are sumptuously illuminated liturgical volumes, featuring a frequently iconic approach to images (see ICON), an opulent use of gold and PURPLE PAGES, and an emphasis on the PATRON. The largely itinerant Ottonian court was instrumental in stimulating the production of manuscripts (principally those of the Liuthar Group), with monastic SCRIPTORIA such as those at Reichenau, Regensburg, and Echternach producing many important illuminated books.

OUTLINE DRAWING

A style of ILLUMINATION in which only the outlines of the figure or object are drawn, in black or colored INK. There appears to have been a classical tradition of outline drawing that was adopted and developed in INSULAR, ANGLO-SAXON, and CAROLINGIAN art. In an illumination, the technique could be used exclusively or in conjunction with FULLY PAINTED elements. Outline drawing

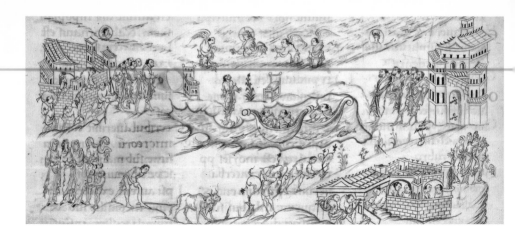

OUTLINE DRAWING
Psalm 106. Harley Psalter. England (Canterbury), early 11th century. 38×31.5 cm (14¹⁵⁄₁₆ × 12⅜ in.).
BL, Ms. Harley 603, fol. 54v (detail).

remained particularly popular in England, although it is occasionally found elsewhere in the West and in BYZANTINE art. It was also frequently employed in the rendering of diagrams. See also TINTED DRAWING.

OVERPAINTING

Overpainting refers to the finished painting that is executed over a drawing or preliminary underpainting. The term also describes the technique of layering paints to extend the color range.

OXIDATION

A chemical reaction resulting from exposure to oxygen. This can cause certain metal-based PIGMENTS (notably silver and white, yellow, or red lead) to fade and/or turn a silver-black and to bleed. A coating of glair (see BINDING MEDIUM) is thought to reduce such tendencies in certain cases, but the conditions in which a manuscript is stored and the length of exposure to adverse atmospheric conditions seem to determine the extent of oxidation.

PALEOGRAPHY

From the Greek *palaiographia*, meaning "ancient writing," paleography is the study of the history of SCRIPTS, their adjuncts (such as ABBREVIATION and punctuation), and their decipherment. The fifteenth-century humanists (see HUMANISTIC) were the first to attempt to distinguish styles of handwriting according to date, but the discipline really began to develop during the second half of the seventeenth century. At this time, Jean Bolland, leader of a group of Flemish Jesuits, was charged by the Holy See with producing an authoritative compendium of SAINTS' LIVES. In the process, the Bollandists established criteria for determining the authenticity of documents through the analysis of script. Jean Mabillon, a Benedictine monk of St. Germain des Près, then published *De re diplomatica* (1681), which includes a section on the history of handwriting and uses paleographic means to argue for the validity of certain ancient grants to the Benedictine Order. Mabillon's principles for assessing the authenticity of documents gave rise to the formal discipline of paleography (or DIPLOMATIC, as it was known until the nineteenth century). Subsequent landmarks in the discipline include the *Nouveau traité de diplomatique* (1750–65) by the Benedictines René-Prosper Tassin and Charles-François Toustain, Charles-François-Bernard de Montfaucon's *Palaeographia graeca* (1708), and the work of Francesco Scipione Maffei of Verona (1675–1755). The twentieth century has witnessed the development of several major schools of paleography, defined by the approaches of key scholars, such as Ludwig Traube and E. A. Lowe.

PALETTE

The range of colors used in a work. The term derives from the name of the flat surface on which paints are sometimes mixed, although shells were more commonly used to contain prepared PIGMENTS during the Middle Ages.

PALIMPSEST

From the Greek *palimpsestos* ("scraped again"), a palimpsest is reused writing support material from which the underlying text has been erased (by washing in the case of PAPYRUS and by using PUMICE or other scraping devices in the case of PARCHMENT). Erasure was not always complete and an underlying text can often be read with the assistance of ultraviolet light.

PANELS

In the context of BINDING, panels are engraved metal blocks used to impress a design on a large part or the whole of a book cover, producing either a blind or gilded impression (see TOOLED). Panels were first used in thirteenth-century Flanders. See also BLOCKED.

PAPER

In the mid-eighth century, the Arabs learned techniques of paper manufacture from the Chinese. The oldest Greek paper manuscripts were produced during the ninth century. Paper (*carta* or *charter*) was made in Muslim Spain beginning in the late eleventh century. During the twelfth and thirteenth centuries, it was used in Italy and the Mediterranean for merchants' notes and by notaries for registers; from the thirteenth century on, paper was actually manufactured in Italy. During the fourteenth and fifteenth centuries, production spread to Switzerland, the Rhineland, and France. In England there was limited production in the fifteenth century; only in the mid-sixteenth century was the paper making industry permanently established. (In the late fifteenth century, the famous publisher William Caxton and his colleagues were still largely importing supplies from Italy and France.)

Correspondence was often written on paper beginning in the fourteenth century, and paper was commonly used in low-grade books from c. 1400 and in legal documents from the sixteenth century (although PARCHMENT also continued to be used). RULING on paper generally consists of FRAME RULING only. The humanists (see HUMANISTIC) revived HARD POINT ruling for a time, but it damaged the paper. In general, INK or LEAD POINT was used for ruling paper CODICES. In early paper books, QUIRES are often protected by parchment outer sheets or GUARDS.

Paper was traditionally made from cotton or linen rags, although more exotic substances such as silk were often employed in the Orient. The rags were soaked and pulverized until reduced to a pulp and were then placed in a vat with a solution of water and size. A wooden frame strung with wires (producing horizontal laid lines and vertical chain lines) was dipped into the mixture and agitated until the fibers fused to form a sheet of paper. This was then placed between sheets of blotting paper and pressed. The paper produced was then either trimmed or left with its rough (deckle) edge. Paper frames often incorporated wire devices (in the form of designs or monograms), which leave an image in the paper known as a watermark. There exist reference volumes containing reproductions of watermarks from broadly datable or localizable contexts, and it is frequently possible to identify watermarks by matching them against such reproductions.

Early paper is generally quite resilient, but beginning in the mid-nineteenth century, when book production increased dramatically, wood and other organic pulps were used (either completely or as additives). These substances introduce a level of acidity into the paper which causes it to turn brown and eventually to crumble away, presenting great difficulties in preservation. Modern acid-free papers are now available.

PAPYRUS

A writing support material made from the papyrus plant, a species of water-grown sedge that grew abundantly in ancient Egypt, where it was used from about 3000 B.C. The outer skin of the stem of the papyrus plant was peeled off and the rest cut into strips that were laid side by side vertically, with another layer of strips then overlaid horizontally. The whole was dampened and beaten or pressed in the sun. The resin released by the fibers during this process fused them into a sheet that was then trimmed and smoothed with PUMICE. The next step was to attach the sheets with a flour paste to form a ROLL. Papyrus was also used for single sheet documents or folded to form CODICES.

The side with the horizontal fibers visible would generally be used for writing with a reed PEN: the horizontal fibers guided the writing on the inner surface, while the vertical fibers strengthened the outside. Papyrus was sturdy and plentiful, and it apparently was rarely reused. There is some indication that trade embargoes during ANTIQUITY led to experiments with other materials, such as PARCHMENT. In fact, in the fourth century, parchment generally replaced papyrus. But it was the collapse of the western Roman Empire and, more significantly, the spread of Islam from the seventh century on, with a consequent reduction of Mediterranean trade, that led to the abandonment of papyrus as an all-purpose writing material. It continued to be used, however, for documents produced in the chanceries of Merovingian Gaul and Ravenna during the sixth and seventh centuries, and the papal chancery used it as an exotic material until the eleventh century.

PARCHMENT

A writing support material that derives its name from Pergamon (Bergama in modern Turkey), an early production center. The term is often used generically to denote animal skin prepared to receive writing, although it is more correctly applied only to sheep and goat skin, with the term *vellum* reserved for calf skin. Uterine vellum, the skin of stillborn or very young calves, is characterized by its small size and particularly fine, white appearance; however, it was rarely used.

To produce parchment or vellum, the animal skins were defleshed in a bath of lime, stretched on a frame, and scraped with a lunular knife while damp. They could then be treated with PUMICE, whitened with a substance such as CHALK, and cut to size. Differences in preparation technique seem to have occasioned greater diversity in appearance than did the type of skin used. Parchment supplanted PAPYRUS as the most popular writing support material in the fourth century, although it was known earlier. Parchment was itself largely replaced by PAPER in the sixteenth century (with the rise of printing), but remained in use for certain high-grade books. See also FLESH SIDE and HAIR SIDE.

PARCHMENTER

A person responsible for making PARCHMENT. Before around 1200, parchment making was presumably conducted largely within monasteries, the primary producers of books. As LAY and commercial production of manuscripts increased, parchmenters often formed a trade group, with shops located in the same part of a town, near the water supply needed for production. See also STATIONER.

PASSIONALE	~~See MARTYROLOGY.~~

PASTEDOWN

A leaf pasted onto the inside of a board (see BOARDS) to conceal the CHANNELING and PEGGING and other mechanics of the BINDING. Pastedowns are often formed of fragments of earlier manuscripts that were considered dispensable.

PATRISTIC

Patristic texts are those written by the Church Fathers or other EARLY CHRISTIAN writers whose authority was particularly respected in later periods. Well-known patristic authors include Saint Augustine, Saint Jerome, and Saint John Chrysostom.

PATRON

The person responsible for commissioning a work. Portraits of patrons are known throughout the Middle Ages, but they grew in popularity beginning in the fourteenth century. See also DONOR. See also the illustration accompanying LECTIONARY.

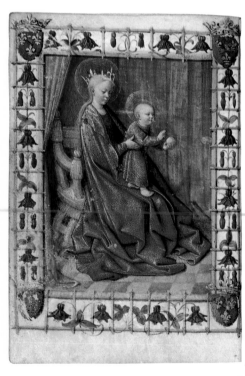 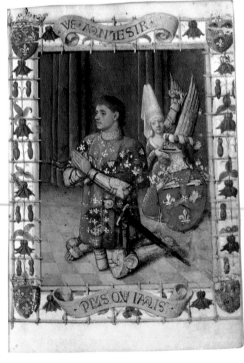

PATRON
Jean Fouquet. *Simon de Varie before the Virgin and Child*. Hours of Simon de Varie. France (Paris or Tours), 1455. Leaf: 11.5×8.2 (4½×3¼ in.). JPGM, Ms. 7 (85.ML.27), fols. 1v–2.

PECIA SYSTEM

A system used from the thirteenth century on, in which university-approved EXEMPLARS of texts were divided into sections and were hired out by STATIONERS to SCRIBES for copying (*pecia* means "piece" in Latin). Not all books, even those for school use, were subject to the pecia system. The sections often carried an abbreviation of the word pecia (for example, p^a) and a numeral, written inconspicuously in the margin.

PEGGING

The securing of CORDS to the BOARDS of a BINDING by means of dowels or pegs, generally of wood.

PEN

A split reed, termed *calamus* in Latin (*qalam* in Arabic), was used to write on PAPYRUS during ANTIQUITY; a frayed reed was used as a BRUSH. These were replaced in the sixth century by the quill pen and animal-hair brushes, which were more flexible and thus better suited for work on PARCHMENT, a tougher material than papyrus. A quill is formed of the flight feather (one of the first five feathers) of the wing of a bird, often a goose—the word pen derives from the Latin for feather, *penna*. The feather was first hardened by heating or by soaking it in water and then immersing it in sand. *Dutching* is a form of curing in which a spatulate tool (dutching hook) is used to manipulate the cooling quill to produce a larger, flatter pen. Nibs were then cut with a KNIFE, the angle of the cuts affecting the appearance of the SCRIPT produced. *Cursive* (i.e., more rapidly written) scripts were generally produced with a thin pen and formal bookscripts with a broad pen. A nib cut at right angles to the shaft produces an informal, *slanted-pen script* in which the heads of letter strokes appear slanted, while a nib cut at an oblique angle to the shaft produces a formal, *straight-pen script* that has horizontal heads to the letter strokes.

PEN-FLOURISHED INITIAL

An INITIAL with a fine linear embellishment, produced with a thin PEN and either text INK or colored inks. Blue and red were generally used during the late ROMANESQUE and GOTHIC periods. Green, common in Anglo-Norman manuscripts, was rarely used after 1200. Violet is found in manuscripts of the final quarter of the thirteenth century virtually everywhere except Paris, and purple occurs during the fourteenth and fifteenth centuries. Pen flourishing can also be applied to other decorative components. See also LITTERA FLORISSA.

PENTATEUCH

The first five books of the Old Testament, which were sometimes incorporated into a single volume.

Pen trial   A test of a newly trimmed PEN nib, termed *probatio pennae* in Latin. A quill pen requires recutting very frequently (at least twice per FOLIO). Catch phrases, names, letters, and sketches were often written in the margins or on FLYLEAVES to test the recut nib, or simply as doodling.

Penwork initial   An ornamental INITIAL produced entirely with a PEN, generally using the same INK as the text. See also PEN-FLOURISHED INITIAL.

Pericope book   See EVANGELARY.

Picture cycle   A series of illustrations of related subject matter that forms a set. One of the commonest types is the PREFATORY CYCLE, which precedes a book's main text. Prefatory cycles are often encountered in PSALTERS. Other illustrative cycles mark the major divisions of a text, such as the scenes from the life of the Virgin in a BOOK OF HOURS or scenes heading the chapters of a ROMANCE or CHRONICLE. Illustrations of the individual subjects of texts, such as those in a BESTIARY or HERBAL, also form a picture cycle.

Pigment   The coloring agent in paint. The paints used in ILLUMINATION consist of vegetable, mineral, and animal extracts, ground or soaked out and mixed with glair as a BINDING MEDIUM, perhaps with some glue and water added. Other additives were also used, including stale urine, honey, and ear wax, to modify color, texture, and opacity; inert whites such as CHALK, eggshell, or white lead were added to increase opacity. Some pigments were obtained locally (such as turnsole, or *crozophora tinctoria*); others were exotic imports (such as ultramarine, made from lapis lazuli imported from Persia or Afghanistan).

During the early Middle Ages, SCRIBES and/or ILLUMINATORS ground and prepared their own pigments, perhaps with the aid of an assistant, but with the growth of specialized, more commercial production around 1200, they often purchased their ingredients in prepared form from a STATIONER or an apothecary. With the rise of experimental science and international trade in the fourteenth century, many colors were added to the traditional PALETTE, which significantly affected styles of illumination. The production of synthetically manufactured pigments (such as mercury-based vermilion and copper blues) and imports (such as saffron yellow from crocus stamens and red lakes from Brazil woods largely imported from Ceylon) increased at this time.

Pigments are difficult to identify precisely without chemical analysis, although other techniques of analysis, such as radiospectroscopy and X-ray fluorescence, as well as reconstructions from medieval recipes, are advancing rapidly. Some pigments also change in a consistent fashion over time: for example, the red lead often used for RUBRICS frequently fades and turns silver-black through OXIDATION, and copper-based verdigris green sometimes eats through the support as it corrodes.

PLUMMET

See LEAD POINT.

PONTIFICAL

A liturgical book containing the order of service for those sacraments administered exclusively by popes or bishops. Among these sacraments are the dedication of churches and altars, the ordination of clergy, confirmation, the blessing of abbots and abbesses and of holy oil, and the consecration of liturgical equipment.

PONTIFICAL

Petrus Lüchter. *Objects Associated with the Consecration of a Church and Altar*. Pontifical. Germany (Constance), 1489. 27.6 × 20.5 cm (10⅞ × 8¹⁄₁₆ in.). JPGM, Ms. Ludwig VII 2 (83.MJ.91), fol. 12v (detail).

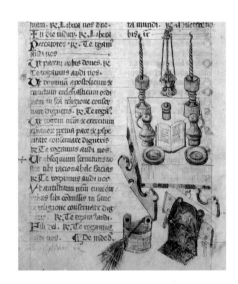

POUNCE

A substance such as CHALK, ash, powdered bone, bread crumbs, or PUMICE that is rubbed into a writing surface in order to improve it. Pounce can reduce greasiness, raise the nap, and whiten PARCHMENT. The term is also used for a post-medieval technique employed in the transfer of an image.

PRAYER BOOK

Collections of prayers for private devotional use appeared at least as early as the eighth century in the INSULAR world and shortly thereafter in the CAROLINGIAN Empire. In ninth-century English illuminated manuscripts, prayers began to be collected according to central devotional themes and were often accompanied by passages from the Gospels and the Psalms. Within the Carolingian and OTTONIAN milieus, series of prayers were often appended to PSALTERS, but without a thematic structure. Throughout the Middle Ages,

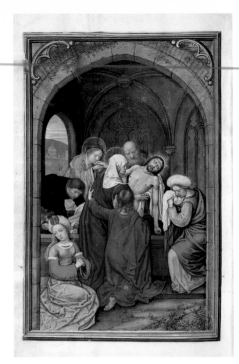
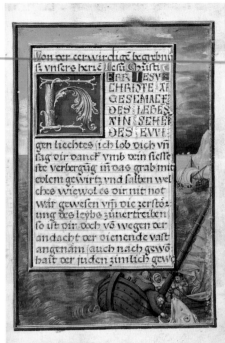

PRAYER BOOK

Simon Bening. *Entombment of Christ; Jonah and the Whale.* Prayer Book of Albrecht of Brandenburg. Belgium (Bruges), 1525–30. Leaf: 16.8 × 11.5 cm (6⅝ × 4½ in.). JPGM, Ms. Ludwig IX 19 (83.ML.115), fols. 328v–329.

prayer books supplemented the psalter and the BOOK OF HOURS as volumes for devotional use. Prayer books grew in popularity during the later Middle Ages, a number containing fine ILLUMINATIONS having been produced for aristocratic PATRONS (such as Charles the Bold, Duke of Burgundy) in the fifteenth century.

PRE-CAROLINGIAN The term embraces the cultures in much of mainland Europe prior to their absorption into the CAROLINGIAN Empire during the late eighth and early ninth centuries. During the pre-Carolingian period, GERMANIC peoples (such as the Franks, Visigoths, Ostrogoths, Lombards, and Burgundians) established a number of successor states throughout what had been the western Roman Empire. Their cultures represented a fusion of pagan Germanic and Christian, or Arian, traditions. Language and SCRIPT underwent a process of vulgarization to some extent, with certain centers (such as Rome, Vivarium, Milan, Seville, Toledo, St. Gall, Bobbio, Luxeuil, and Corbie) attempting to preserve elements of the learning and culture of late ANTIQUITY. The pre-Carolingian period also saw the increasing application of ornament to text and the development of the decorated letter.

PRE-CAROLINGIAN

PRE-CAROLINGIAN
Text page. Gregory the
Great, *Moralia in Job*.
France (Laon?), 8th
century. 26.2 × 17.5 cm
(10⁵⁄₁₆ × 6⅞ in.). BL, Add.
Ms. 31031, fol. 1 (detail).

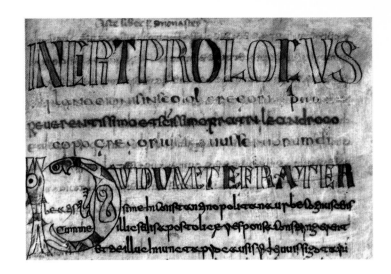

Pre-Carolingian is used in a more specific context when refer-
ring to the culture of Gaul from the fifth to the eighth century—
that is, Merovingian Gaul before the Carolingian period.

PREFATORY CYCLE   A series of MINIATURES that introduce a text. The prefatory cycle
in manuscript PSALTERS reached a developed form in ANGLO-SAXON

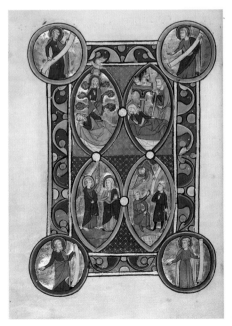
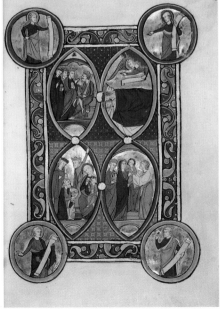

PREFATORY CYCLE
Tree of Jesse and *Scenes from the Infancy of Christ*. Psalter. France (Paris), c. 1250–60.
Leaf: 19.2 × 13.4 cm (7⁹⁄₁₆ × 5¼ in.). JPGM, Ms. Ludwig VIII 4 (83.MK.95), fols. 22v–23.

England in the mid-eleventh century (the Tiberius Psalter). Psalter cycles usually consist of scenes from the life of Christ or of King David, author of many of the Psalms.

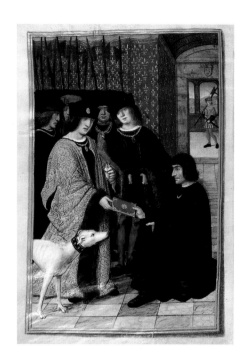

PRESENTATION MINIATURE

A MINIATURE depicting the presentation of a book to its PATRON or DONOR. Strictly speaking, the presentation miniature appears only in the presentation copy of a text, but such images frequently entered into the decorative program and would be included in subsequent copies (in which case the term *dedication miniature* is preferable). Although encountered earlier, presentation miniatures became popular during the fifteenth century.

PRICKING

The marking of a FOLIO or BIFOLIUM by a point or KNIFE to guide RULING. The term also refers to the series of marks that resulted. Pricking was generally conducted before the bifolia were folded to form a QUIRE. In INSULAR manuscript production, however, pricking was done after folding. Templates were occasionally used.

PRIMER

Alternative English name for a BOOK OF HOURS.

PROBATIO PENNAE (pl. PROBATIONES PENNAE)

See PEN TRIAL.

PROGRAM	See PICTURE CYCLE.
PROVENANCE	Provenance is the history of a book's ownership. Provenance information may be deduced from evidence relating to the original commission (such as HERALDRY, EMBLEMS, DEVICES, and MOTTOES), from subsequent additions and annotations (including OBITS, inscriptions, bookplates, and library labeling), or from references in catalogues, correspondence, and other records.
PSALTER	The psalter is the Book of Psalms. Medieval manuscripts of the Psalms were used in liturgical as well as private devotional contexts and often contained ancillary texts such as a CALENDAR, Canticles, creeds, a LITANY OF THE SAINTS, and prayers.

Psalters designed for use in the performance of the DIVINE OFFICE often contain other relevant texts, such as the Hours of the Virgin. The psalter was the principal book for private devotions before the emergence of the BOOK OF HOURS in the thirteenth century. The Psalms also formed a major part of many medieval PRAYER BOOKS from the ninth century on. In the non-monastic

PSALTER
The Crucifixion; initial *A* with *Clerics and Laymen in Prayer*; *Saint Christina Cast into the Sea and Rescued by Angels* (in the bas-de-page). Queen Mary Psalter. England (London?), c. 1310–20. 27.5 × 17.5 cm (10¹³⁄₁₆ × 6⅞ in.). BL, Royal Ms. 2.B.VII, fol. 256v.

Roman LITURGY of the Middle Ages, all one hundred and fifty Psalms were recited each week, the majority at matins and vespers. The cycle began at matins on Sunday with Psalm 1 and continued at matins on the following days: Psalm 26 was the first recited on Monday, Psalm 38 the first on Tuesday, Psalm 52 the first on Wednesday, Psalm 68 the first on Thursday, Psalm 80 the first on Friday, Psalm 97 the first on Saturday. The cycle for vespers commenced on Sunday with Psalm 109 and continued throughout the week with the remaining Psalms (some Psalms were set aside for other hours). Other divisions of the Psalms are occasionally found, such as the Irish division of the three fifties (beginning at Psalms 1, 51, and 101). Such divisions would often be given prominence within the decorative program.

Depictions of King David, author of many of the Psalms, frequently introduce the psalter (especially as historiated *Beatus* initials to Psalm 1), and PREFATORY CYCLES were often added, along with an illuminated calendar. BYZANTINE psalter illustration exerted an important influence on the West.

PUMICE

Volcanic glass, used in its powdered form as POUNCE on PARCHMENT; in its consolidated form, it was employed to scrape parchment for reuse as a PALIMPSEST.

PURPLE PAGES

Sheets of PARCHMENT dyed or painted purple, as a background for ILLUMINATION or for SCRIPT in gold or silver (see CHRYSOGRAPHY). Purple pages were introduced into high-grade book production during the LATE ANTIQUE and EARLY CHRISTIAN periods as marks of costliness and luxury and sometimes to imbue a work with imperial connotations (from the Greek *porphyrogenitus*, or "born in the purple," used of children born to reigning BYZANTINE emperors). Several important liturgical volumes made in the INSULAR, ANGLO-SAXON, CAROLINGIAN, and OTTONIAN worlds employed purple pages, and they enjoyed a revival during the RENAISSANCE. In Mediterranean regions, murex purple (a shellfish dye) was often used, but in northwestern Europe alternatives such as the plant-dye folium (from the turnsole, or *crozophora tinctoria*) seem to have been more frequently employed.

PUTTO
(pl. PUTTI)

A nude infant, usually depicted with wings, popular in RENAISSANCE art as a means of enriching the decorative quality of a work.

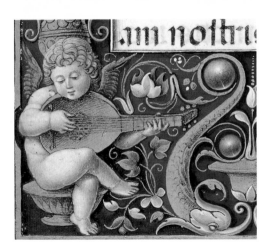

QUARTO

The word refers to a medium-size volume, one quarter the area of a full sheet of writing material.

QUIRE

Quires are the "gatherings" or "booklets" of which a book is formed. Quire numeration, which began in the LATE ANTIQUE period, consists of numbers written on a quire (usually on its final VERSO) to facilitate arrangement during BINDING.

Quire signatures (or leaf signatures) are numbers and/or letters written in a quire to facilitate the arrangement of its internal components. These were at first ad hoc, but beginning around 1400 they might follow a system: for example, ai-aiv could be written on the first four leaves of the first quire; bi-biv on the first four leaves of the second quire, and so on. Such annotations only became widespread from the late thirteenth century on. See also BIFOLIUM, FOLIO, and CODICOLOGY.

RECTO

The front side of a FOLIO or leaf, abbreviated as *r* and sometimes denoted as *a*.

REGISTER

A horizontal tier. Full-page MINIATURES containing several scenes were sometimes divided into registers. See the illustration accompanying CAROLINGIAN.

RENAISSANCE

A French term meaning "rebirth" and applied to a revival of the arts and learning stimulated by an interest in the past. Although we speak of the CAROLINGIAN, Northumbrian, and twelfth-century renaissances, the term by itself denotes a two-hundred-

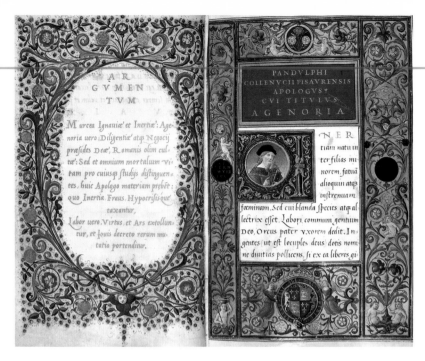

RENAISSANCE

Ludovico degli Arrighi (scribe) and Attavante degli Attavanti (illuminator). Initial *I* with *Bust of a Man*.
Pandulfo Collenuccio of Pesaro, *Apologi*. Italy (Rome and Florence), 1509–47.
Leaf: 18 × 13 cm (7 1/16 × 5 1/8 in.). BL, Ms. Royal 12.C.VIII, fols. 3v–4.

year period, from approximately the mid-fourteenth to the mid-sixteenth century, that marks a transition from the Middle Ages to the modern era and is characterized by the revival of the learning of classical ANTIQUITY. Renaissance (originally the Italian *rinascimento*) was coined by Italian humanists (see HUMANISTIC), who saw their own age as significantly different from the preceding one, which they perceived as GOTHIC. Working initially in centers such as Florence and Rome, the humanists began to study CLASSICAL TEXTS, although many of the copies available to them dated no earlier than Carolingian times. In the art of the period, we find a noticeable concern with NATURALISTIC rendering and the use of classical motifs.

A love of decoration remained a feature of Renaissance ILLUMINATION, but the GROTESQUES of medieval art were replaced by PUTTI, classical masks, vases, jewels, and other motifs. MINIATURES increasingly reflected the advanced styles of easel and fresco painters (the famous sixteenth-century illuminator Giulio Clovio was known as "the little Michelangelo"). Humanist scholars such as Petrarch (1304–1374) and Poggio Bracciolini (1380–1459) were themselves involved in book production, and their reforms of SCRIPT and promotion of literacy were to play an important role in the early development of printing. Secular patronage was a significant factor in Renaissance book production: kings, princes, and other nobles no less than popes and ecclesiastical leaders throughout Europe used the arts to promote their political and economic status. See also the illustrations accompanying PUTTO and WHITE VINE-STEM.

RINCEAUX

A form of ornament commonly used in BORDERS during the fourteenth and fifteenth centuries. It consists of a patterning of fine foliate branches.

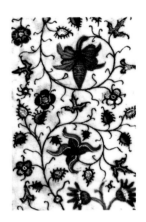

RINCEAUX
Workshop of the Boucicaut Master. *The Visitation.* Balfour Hours. France (Paris), c. 1415–20. 20.4 × 14.9 cm (8¹⁄₁₆ × 5⅞ in.). JPGM, Ms. 22 (86.ML.571), fol. 48 (full page and detail of border).

RITUAL

A manual containing the prayers and formulae for the administration of all the sacraments (except the Eucharist), such as baptism and extreme unction.

ROLL

The roll (*rotulus* or *volumen*) was, along with the TABLET, the principal vehicle for writing during ANTIQUITY. Rolls were originally formed of sheets of PAPYRUS pasted together and were stored in *capsae*, cylindrical boxes resembling Victorian hat boxes. They were unrolled horizontally from left to right, with about four columns of text visible at any one time. Information concerning author, text, and production (the COLOPHON) served to label the roll, along with the INCIPIT and EXPLICIT inscriptions. The drawbacks of the roll form in terms of portability and cross-referencing led

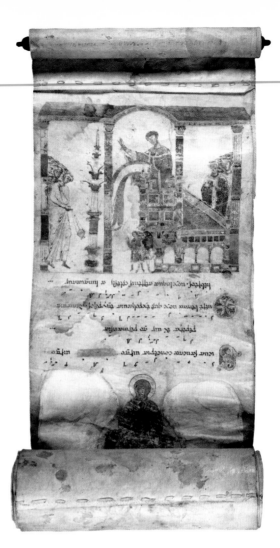

Roll

The Blessing of the Paschal Candle. Exultet roll. Italy (Monte Cassino), late 11th century. 785 × 27.5 cm (309 1/16 × 10 13/16 in.). BL, Add. Ms. 30337.

to its general replacement by the CODEX in the fourth century. The roll survived, however, throughout the Middle Ages, fulfilling certain specialized functions—although it was now made of PARCHMENT (sewn or glued together) and was read vertically. Such forms were useful for storing lengthy records and thus were frequently used for administrative purposes (such as Exchequer Rolls). Rolls also carried genealogies and pedigrees, and some of these manuscripts were finely illuminated. Roll CHRONICLES often accompanied royal genealogies. Illuminated Exultet rolls, with texts for the blessing of the Easter candle, were designed for public viewing, with the text facing the reader and the image placed upside down in relation to the text, to face the congregation over the lectern. Prayer rolls also survive; they may have been carried as amulets.

ROMAN NUMERALS

The system of conveying numerical information, generally employed throughout ANTIQUITY and the Middle Ages, in which quantities are represented as Roman letters: I or i (1), V or v (5), X or x (10), L or l (50), C or c (100), D or d (500), M or m (1000). There were local variations, which included the use of other letters. See also ARABIC NUMERALS.

ROMANCE

A genre of literature that developed in the twelfth and thirteenth centuries in France. The Old French word *romanz* originally denoted texts in the French VERNACULAR but later came to be applied to narrative tales of the deeds of noblemen and noblewomen. Romances were frequently illustrated, sometimes modestly, but often lavishly if the PATRON was wealthy. The combination of imaginative stories of chivalric love and heroism with details from everyday courtly life (which abound in the illustrations) contributed to the popularity of the romance, as did the rise in secular literacy and patronage.

Most examples of the romance can be termed *romans d'aventures* ("chivalric romances"), since their major theme is hazardous adventure. Early romances are generally in verse, but prose romances (such as the French Arthurian cycle) also proliferated. Among the earliest romances are those written in the later twelfth

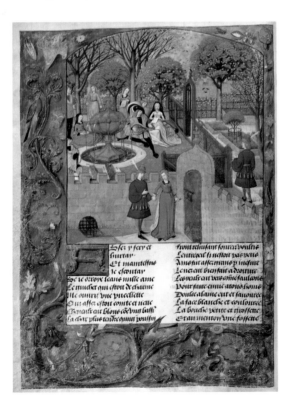

ROMANCE
The Lover Admitted into the Garden. Guillaume de Lorris and Jean de Meun, *Roman de la rose.* Belgium (Bruges?), c. 1490–1500. 39.4 × 29.2 cm (15½ × 11½ in.). BL, Harley Ms. 4425, fol. 12v.

century by Chrétien de Troyes, who transformed mere incident into meaningful action by stressing moral themes, as in *Erec et Enide*, one of his first works in the genre. Although fictional, romances were often based on historical events, either classical (*King Alisaunder*) or medieval (*Lai d'Haveloc* and *Le Morte Arthur*). Love—as perceived in a rigid system of chivalric behavior—often plays a role in French works, one of the most popular being the *Roman de la rose*, begun by Guillaume de Lorris (c. 1237) and completed by Jean de Meun (c. 1275), which combines the allegorical and satirical with courtly love and human emotions.

ROMANESQUE

The term Romanesque was applied in the nineteenth century to Western architecture of the late eleventh and twelfth centuries (the precise span varies from region to region) because of its use of Roman principles of construction. Romanesque is also applied

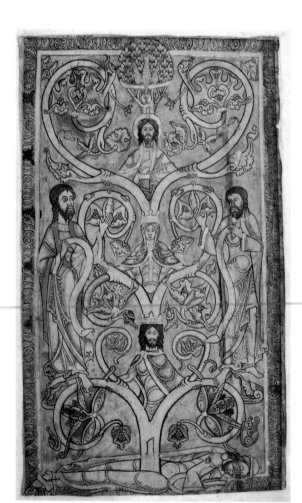

ROMANESQUE
Tree of Jesse. Psalter of Henry of Blois. England (Winchester), 1140–60. 32.5 × 22.5 cm (12¹³⁄₁₆ × 8⅞ in.). BL, Cotton Ms. Nero C.IV, fol. 9.

to the other visual arts of the period to indicate a style that drew on earlier art of the West, including that of ancient Rome, and also incorporated BYZANTINE and even some Islamic influences. Although there are regional flavors within Romanesque art, it was essentially an international style that promoted an interest in the human figure, an interest that was, nevertheless, subordinated to decorative forms and patterns (as seen in DAMP-FOLD drapery). A taste for the humorous and GROTESQUE is also manifest, combining with the decorative to produce characteristic ZOOMORPHIC, ANTHROPOMORPHIC, GYMNASTIC, INHABITED, and HISTORIATED INITIALS, ultimately of INSULAR and PRE-CAROLINGIAN derivation. The number of subjects depicted in religious art during this period increased, stimulated by religious reforms and scholarship, resulting in an expanded Old and New Testament ICONOGRAPHY (with developments in areas such as TYPOLOGY). Although the production and patronage of manuscripts was principally ecclesiastical in the Romanesque period, there was also an increase in the production of illuminated scholarly and technical works, such as BESTIARIES and HERBALS.

RUBRIC

A title, chapter heading, or instruction that is not strictly part of the text but which helps to identify its components. Red INK was often used to distinguish such elements, hence the term, which derives from the Latin for red, *rubrica*.

RUBRICATOR

A person responsible for supplying the RUBRICS within a manuscript. Rubrication—sometimes done by the SCRIBE—generally followed the laying out and writing of the text.

RULING

The process by which a frame and/or horizontal lines are produced to guide the hand in writing; the word also refers to the linear guide thus produced. Ruling was guided by PRICKING. Beginning in the CAROLINGIAN period, templates were sometimes used in pricking and ruling. Before the late eleventh century, ruling was generally executed with a HARD POINT, producing a ridge-and-furrow effect. Thereafter LEAD POINT was used in the layout of individual pages, enabling greater flexibility. When the thin PEN used to produce cursive SCRIPTS was revived in the later twelfth century, ruling was also done in INK, especially from the late thirteenth century on. Colored inks were employed in some manuscripts, such as the pink ruling in fifteenth-century BOOKS OF HOURS. The Italian humanists (see HUMANISTIC) revived the use of hard point for ruling. When PAPER was used as the writing support material, this could result in tears in the paper. See also MISE-EN-PAGE.

Running title

A line of text at the head of a FOLIO that identifies the title of a work or one of its subsections. Running titles (also called *running heads*) help the reader find the different parts of a manuscript.

Run-over symbol

A decorative device (abstract, foliate, zoomorphic, or anthropomorphic) which indicates that the text of a line has been carried over to occupy the remainder of the line above or below, a space that otherwise would have been left blank. Run-over symbols serve both decorative and space-saving functions, especially in verse forms such as the Psalms, and were initially popularized in INSULAR and PRE-CAROLINGIAN art.

Sacramentary

A SERVICE BOOK containing the prayers recited by the celebrant during high MASS (collect, secret, postcommunion, and the canon of the mass). The other parts of the mass are contained in the GOSPEL BOOK or EVANGELARY, the EPISTOLARY, and the GRADUAL. The texts of the sacramentary are divided into the unchanging elements (the canon and ordinary of the mass) and the variable texts, the latter arranged according to the liturgical year. Further divisions are the Common of Saints (standard formulae for saints who were not accorded individual services) and votive masses for special occasions, such as marriage. The *Te igitur* and *Vere dignum* openings were principal vehicles for ILLUMINATION.

Several distinct rites were current in the West before c. 700, the two most influential being the Roman and the Gallican. The former was followed in Rome and southern Italy and the latter in much of the rest of Western Europe. By 700 the Roman sacramentary had reached Gaul, where it was modified by Gallican usage. This mixture of rites resulted in the Gelasian Sacramentary (spuriously attributed to the late fifth-century Pope Gelasius I). As part of his efforts to standardize church ritual in the CAROLINGIAN period, Charlemagne asked Pope Hadrian I to provide an authentic Roman sacramentary for use throughout the empire. In 785–86, the pope sent the emperor the *Sacramentarium Hadrianum*, also known as the Gregorian Sacramentary. This, however, was a special sacramentary for papal use. In order to adapt it for general use, scholars such as Alcuin of York and Benedict of Aniane added supplementary material drawn from the Gallican and Gelasian rites. By the late thirteenth century, the sacramentary had virtually been replaced by the MISSAL. See the illustration accompanying OTTONIAN.

Saints' lives

Narratives of the lives (*vitae*) of the saints formed a popular genre from the early Middle Ages on. As holy figures continued to be

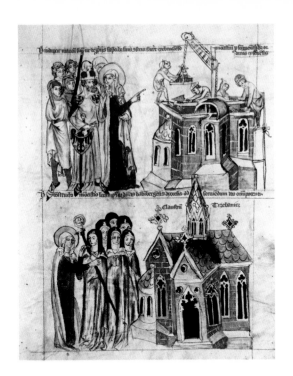

canonized throughout the Middle Ages, new lives were composed
and translations were made into the VERNACULAR. Many of the
early lives were incorporated into the MARTYROLOGY for use as
readings in the DIVINE OFFICE. Hagiography (the biography of
saints) formed an essential part of the ecclesiastical library and
was also a popular source for reading among the laity.

SANCTORALE

The celebration of saints' feasts, except for those falling between
December 24 and January 13, also known as the Proper of Saints.
The term sanctorale also refers to the section of a liturgical book
containing the texts for those celebrations. Because the saints'
feasts falling between December 24 and January 13 were so
closely identified with the Christmas season, they were included in
the TEMPORALE, usually a separate section in medieval liturgical
manuscripts. The Common of Saints is another separate section,
giving formulae for the saints not accorded individual services in
the sanctorale or temporale. For the MASS, the temporale, sanctorale, and Common of Saints (along with votive masses for special
occasions) provide the annual cycle of variable elements, the
invariables being the canon and ordinary of the mass.

SCHOOL BOOK

A book made for use in teaching within an ecclesiastical or university context. School books can be identified from annotations

and other markings made for study purposes. Their production increased greatly with the rise of universities around 1200. STATIONERS emerged as the chief purveyors of such works, which were often (but not necessarily) quite modestly and cheaply produced, sometimes using the PECIA SYSTEM. The subjects of school books varied, from biblical and PATRISTIC works and COMMENTARIES, to treatises on grammar, mathematics, astronomy, legal texts (see DECRETALS and DIGEST), MEDICAL TEXTS, and CLASSICAL TEXTS.

SCHOOL OF ILLUMINATION

A group of artists whose work is stylistically related. Because the identification of individual ILLUMINATORS can be very difficult, the decoration of a given manuscript will often be attributed to a school of illumination. Not a school or academy in the modern sense, a school of illumination is most commonly named after a place where the works were produced (for example, the Ghent-Bruges School) or after a particularly important or representative manuscript (such as the Queen Mary Group, named after the Queen Mary PSALTER). See the illustration accompanying PSALTER.

SCRIBE

A person engaged in the physical writing of books or documents. A number of scribes were also artists. In ANTIQUITY, scribes and notaries constituted a professional class. During the EARLY CHRISTIAN period and the Middle Ages, they often worked within an

SCRIBE

Vincent of Beauvais in His Study. Vincent of Beauvais, *Speculum historiale.* Belgium (Bruges?), c. 1478–83. 52.5 × 33 cm (20¹¹⁄₁₆ × 13 in.). BL, Royal Ms. 14.E.I (part 1), fol. 3 (detail).

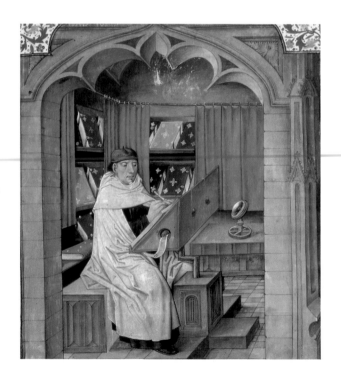

ecclesiastical SCRIPTORIUM as part of a team, or were attached to a court or an official chancery (a record office). Documents continued to be produced by independent scribes in certain areas, although to a very limited extent. Following the rise of the universities around 1200, scribes began to function independently, living alongside each other in urban centers and sometimes joining minor clerical orders. Both men and women served as scribes, and occasionally authors were themselves competent scribes (for example, Petrarch and Christine de Pizan in the fourteenth and early fifteenth centuries, respectively). Scribes sometimes employed assistants or colleagues on a project. They could even be attached to individual households. See also MONASTIC PRODUCTION and SECULAR PRODUCTION. See also the illustration accompanying GOSPEL BOOK.

SCRIPT   The handwriting used in manuscripts. Medieval script was subject to greater discipline and more rigid rules and hierarchies than modern personal handwriting, for in early book production such professional or semi-professional handwriting had to serve many of the functions of modern print. The form and function of a book determined the overall appearance of a script—its *aspect*—the speed and care with which the letters were formed—its *ductus*—and the number of space-saving devices employed (notably ABBREVIATIONS). Seldom was the same grade of script used for, say, a liturgical manuscript and a document or SCHOOL BOOK. The cut and thickness of the PEN nib alters the appearance and degree of formality of a script; and writing materials generally influenced the development of letter forms. Majuscule scripts employ what can be thought of as "uppercase" letters and are of generally even height. This script is also termed *bilinear*, because the letters are confined between two horizontal lines. Minuscule scripts are "lowercase," with longer strokes (ascenders and descenders) that extend above and below the body of the letter (as in *d* and *q*) and touch on four lines (*quadrilinear* script).

Initially majuscule scripts, comprising square and rustic capitals, uncials, and half-uncials, were used for more formal purposes than minuscule, but with the development of Caroline minuscule in CAROLINGIAN scriptoria in the late eighth century, even formal scripts were minuscules. The degree of formality now lay in the speed and care with which a script was written. *Set scripts* were slowly and carefully produced, with the SCRIBE frequently lifting the pen from the writing surface. *Cursive scripts* were written more rapidly with less lifting and sometimes include loops. *Current scripts* were the most rapidly written and informal and are often difficult to read. The more formal text scripts are generally termed *formal book script*, *textualis*, or *textura* (or variations such as

Gothic black-letter script), while the less formal are termed *cursives*. The fusion of the formal and cursive styles gave rise to *hybrid* or *bastard* scripts.

Beginning around 1400, the humanists (see HUMANISTIC) sought to reform medieval scripts, and in so doing laid the foundation for many early typefaces.

SCRIPTORIUM
(pl. SCRIPTORIA)

A writing room. The term is generally (but not exclusively) used of the place in a monastery or church where books are made.

SECULAR PRODUCTION

Book production was a secular activity during ANTIQUITY, but from the EARLY CHRISTIAN period until the rise of the universities around 1200, it was largely conducted in ecclesiastical SCRIPTORIA. There is evidence, however, of continuing secular activity during the early Middle Ages, notably around St. Gall in Switzerland. It has also been suggested that secular itinerant artists participated in MONASTIC PRODUCTION. In addition, SCRIBES were attached to secular courts and households. With the growth in more specialized and commercialized book production after 1200, ILLUMINATORS, scribes, and the STATIONERS who supplied their materials and subcontracted work were usually LAY members of society— both men and women—although many were clerics in minor orders. Scribes, illuminators, stationers, and PARCHMENTERS often lived in the same urban neighborhood and worked together on individual projects (see PECIA SYSTEM) or more regularly as part of a WORKSHOP. From the early Middle Ages on, secular people, usually aristocrats, participated in book production as PATRONS or as authors, some of them (such as Christine de Pizan in the early fifteenth century) actually copying their own works, a trend which flourished among the HUMANISTIC authors.

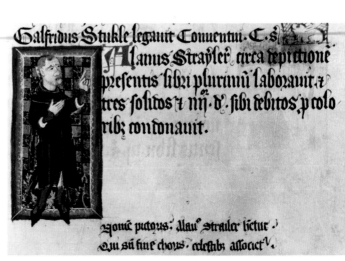

SECULAR PRODUCTION
Alan Strayler. *Self-Portrait.*
Book of the Benefactors of
St. Alban's Abbey. England
(St. Albans), 1380. 36.5×23
cm (14⅜×9¹⁄₁₆ in.). BL,
Cotton Ms. Nero D.VII,
fol. 108 (detail).

The text next to the artist's self-portrait announces that he has donated to the abbey the cost of the pigments he used in this work.

SECUNDO FOLIO   The opening words of the second FOLIO of a manuscript. Since these words differ from one copy of a text to another, depending on the size of the SCRIPT and folio, the secundo folio is often cited when cataloguing manuscripts, a practice that originated in the Middle Ages in order to distinguish individual copies of a text in a way that its opening words could not.

SEQUENTIARY   A book (or portion of a GRADUAL or TROPER) containing sequences (extended melodies) sung by a soloist between the alleluia and the Gospel lesson at MASS.

SERVICE BOOK   A book used in the performance of the Christian LITURGY.

SEWING ON SUPPORTS   The process of linking the QUIRES of a manuscript into book form by sewing them on to CORDS. This is the usual form of medieval BINDING.

SEWING STATIONS   The points in the GUTTER where the sewing needle travels through the fold to the outer edge of the SPINE in order to attach the QUIRE to the CORDS or to another quire.

SGRAFFITO   Sgraffito is writing produced by scratching through a top layer of paint to reveal the underlying PIGMENT or writing surface.

SHELF MARK   A mark, often incorporating numbers, which indicates a book's location within a library. The shelf mark is frequently the designation by which individual manuscripts are known.

SHOULDER   The place where one of the BOARDS of a book joins the SPINE.

SIGNE-DE-RENVOI   Literally a "sign of return," a signe-de-renvoi is a graphic symbol marking a place where a correction or insertion is to be made. A corresponding symbol, usually written in the margin, introduces the corrected text or insertion. A signe-de-renvoi may also mark a cross-reference.

SINGLETON   A single FOLIO that has lost its mate (the other half of the BIFOLIUM) or that originally was designed to be sewn into a book as a single sheet. The latter situation could occur when the layout of the book did not require a text or image to follow immediately at that point, or when that folio carried work, such as a MINIATURE, which was executed by a separate member of the work team.

SPINE

The edge at which a book is sewn together. Rounded, glued spines that were hammered into shape were first introduced in the early sixteenth century. Prior to this, spines were flat, apart from the raised CORDS. Spines sometimes carry protective extensions at either end known as *end tabs*.

STAMPED

See TOOLED.

STAPLE

A metal fitting attaching the chain to one of the BOARDS of a CHAINED BOOK, usually at its HEAD.

STATIONER

Following the rise of the universities around 1200, the growth in SECULAR PRODUCTION and in consumer demand led to increasing specialization and commercialization in book production. A group of middlemen, known as stationers (*cartolai* in Italy, *libraires* in France), emerged. They supplied materials to craftsmen and received and subcontracted commissions, often with formal recognition from the universities. This decentralization stimulated new techniques of book production, such as the systematic marking up of leaves and QUIRES for assembly by the stationer and the provision of INSTRUCTIONS. See also PECIA SYSTEM.

STEMMA
(pl. STEMMATA)

The reconstruction of the "family tree" of a text or program of ILLUMINATION, designed to indicate relationships among manuscripts and the existence of possible intermediary EXEMPLARS.

STRAP AND PIN

A device for keeping a book closed and preventing the distortion of its shape. The strap-and-pin mechanism, known from before 1200, consists of a small metal plate with a raised pin placed at the center of one of the BOARDS; a long leather strap attached to the other board ends in a pierced metal tab designed to slot onto the corresponding pin. The use of two strap-and-pin mechanisms is characteristic of BINDINGS from the fourteenth century on in England and slightly earlier on the Continent. The pin was on the lower board in England and occasionally in France, but it was usually on the upper board on the Continent. Strap-and-pin mechanisms continued to be used into the early modern period. See also CLASP.

STYLIZED

The stylized rendering of a painted subject is governed by non-naturalistic decorative conventions.

STYLUS
(pl. STYLI)

A pointed implement, generally of metal or bone, used for writing on wax TABLETS. A stylus can also be used for PRICKING and RULING a manuscript. Some styli have triangular heads which, when heated, are used to smooth wax for reuse.

SUFFRAGE

An intercessory prayer, sometimes called a *memorial*, addressed to a saint. A suffrage is preceded by an antiphon, a versicle, and a response, and may occur during the DIVINE OFFICE. Suffrages of saints are often included in BOOKS OF HOURS, where they are presented according to a hierarchy, beginning with the Trinity and often followed by the Virgin, Saint Michael, Saint John the Baptist, the apostles, martyrs, confessors, and female saints. The particular saints appearing in a group of suffrages vary according to region or personal devotions. Suffrages are known to have existed from at least the eleventh century (although the earliest extant manuscripts date from the thirteenth century).

TABLET

Tablets of wood, or sometimes ivory, were used as writing surfaces in two ways: either INK was applied on them; or they were hollowed out and filled with wax so that one could write with a STYLUS. Along with the ROLL, the tablet was the principal writing vehicle during ANTIQUITY, being used for informal purposes, teaching, letters, drafting, and for records (such as letters of citizenship). The gradual substitution of sheets of PARCHMENT for wood or ivory may well have stimulated the development of the CODEX form. Tablets continued to be used into the twentieth century for informal financial accounts (by French fishermen, for example). During the Middle Ages, they fulfilled a variety of functions: drafting texts; trying out artistic designs; recording liturgical commemorations; note taking during study; accounting and legal contexts; as proto-Filofaxes; and as love tokens filled with amorous poetry. Tablets ranged in format from robust teaching tablets to portable GIRDLE BOOKS. Although different colors of wax were used, black and green predominated. A number of tablets were sometimes bound together with leather thongs or within a leather case. Tablets were also made with handles (the *tabula ansata*), whose shape could serve as a decorative motif. See the illustration accompanying BENEDICTIONAL.

TAIL

The foot or lower end of a manuscript.

TAILPIECE	A panel of ornament, sometimes containing a RUBRIC or COLOPHON, which stands at the end of a text. See also HEADPIECE.
TANNED	Tanning is the process of manufacturing leather by soaking animal skin in tannin, an acidic substance made from tree bark, GALLNUTS, or a similar plant source. Tanning gives the leather a red-brown coloration.
TE IGITUR PAGE	See MISSAL and SACRAMENTARY.
TEMPORALE	The celebration of christological feasts (including Christmas, Easter, Ascension, and Pentecost) and the section of a liturgical book containing the texts for those feasts. The temporale also includes the saints' feast days celebrated between December 24 and January 13 because of their close association with the Christmas season. For the MASS, the temporale, together with the SANCTORALE, the Common of Saints, and the invariable canon and ordinary of the mass, provides the order of services for the liturgical year.
THONGS	See CORDS.
TINTED DRAWING	A style of ILLUMINATION in which the outlines of the subject are drawn in black or colored INK and tints of colored wash are

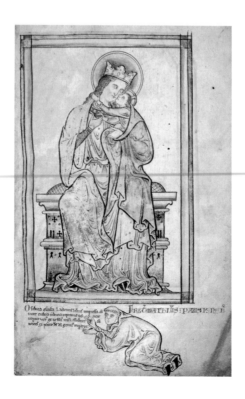

TINTED DRAWING
Matthew Paris. *Matthew Paris before the Virgin and Child*. Matthew Paris, *Historia Anglorum*. England (St. Albans), 1250–59. 35.8×25 cm (14⅛×9¹³⁄₁₆ in.). BL, Royal Ms. 14.C.VII, fol. 6.

applied to all or some of the surfaces to suggest modeling. Tinted drawing was particularly popular in ANGLO-SAXON England and enjoyed a revival in thirteenth-century England in the work of Matthew Paris and the Court School of Henry III. The technique is sometimes used in conjunction with FULLY PAINTED elements. See also OUTLINE DRAWING.

TIRONIAN

See ABBREVIATION.

TITLE PIECE

A decorative panel or page carrying the title of a work, or a label on a BINDING. The positioning and style of a title piece can reveal a great deal about PROVENANCE and methods of library storage.

TONARY

A book in which antiphons, responsories, and other chants of the MASS and DIVINE OFFICE are classified according to the eight musical modes. Independent tonaries first appear in the CAROLINGIAN period but are rare. The tonary is more often incorporated into liturgical books, such as the ANTIPHONAL, the GRADUAL, and the TROPER.

TOOLED

Tooling is the decoration of a surface with the aid of metal hand tools and stamps (a technique employing the latter being termed *stamped*). On BINDINGS, the tools were used to impress the decoration into the leather covering, which was often dampened. The impression or indentation produced is called *blind* if it remains uncolored. Gold tooling became popular in the fifteenth century. In this process, gold leaf was laid onto a coating of glair and impressed into the leather with a heated tool, leaving an image in gold after the excess was rubbed away. Gilded surfaces (see GILDING) in ILLUMINATION were also sometimes tooled.

TRANSITIONAL STYLE

The term refers to the style practiced in European art from about 1180 to 1220, that is, in the period of transition between the ROMANESQUE and the GOTHIC. The most notable characteristic of this art is its stylistic experimentation, partly stimulated by a heightened interest in BYZANTINE art, as in the work of some of the illuminators of the Winchester BIBLE. The Transitional Style also shows a shift from some of the more decorative, MANNERED effects of Romanesque art toward a greater degree of NATURALISTIC rendering. See illustration on next page.

TROMPE L'OEIL

A French expression meaning "deceives the eye," trompe l'oeil describes painting in which things are made to appear to be resting on or projecting from the surface of the picture. See the illustration accompanying BORDER.

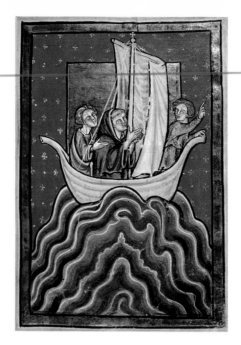

TROPER

A book containing tropes, that is, musical and textual additions to the chants of the MASS or DIVINE OFFICE. Tropers are known from the early Middle Ages on.

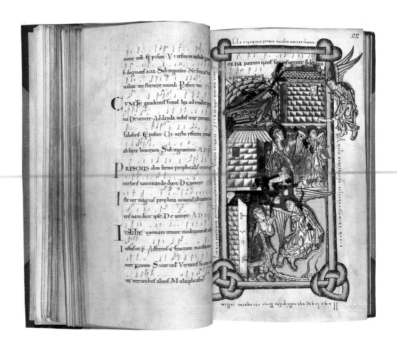

TROPER

An Angel Releases Saint Peter from Prison. Caligula Troper. England (Hereford, Worcester, or Canterbury?), c. 1050. Leaf: 21.6 × 13.2 cm (8½ × 5³⁄₁₆ in.). BL, Cotton Ms. Caligula A.XIV, fols. 21v–22.

TURN-INS

The edges of the covering material of a BINDING, which are folded over the HEAD, TAIL, and FORE EDGE of the BOARDS and secured to their inner sides.

TYPOLOGY

Typology is an interpretive system in Christian thought wherein people, events, and passages of the Old Testament are seen as prefigurations of New Testament themes. The system is designed to prove that the New Testament is a fulfillment of the Old. The sacrifice of Isaac, for example, foretells the Crucifixion; David is a type of Christ; and the stories of Jonah and the whale and Daniel in the lions' den prefigure Christ's Passion and Resurrection. Although encountered during the early Middle Ages, typological juxtapositions become more frequent in art from the eleventh century on. See also BIBLE MORALISÉE and BIBLIA PAUPERUM.

UNDERDRAWING

Preliminary drawing that lies under the final painted or inked image. Prior to the eleventh century, underdrawing was often executed with a HARD POINT, but thereafter a METAL POINT, especially a LEAD POINT, or diluted INK was generally used. STYLI, dividers, and compasses were sometimes employed in the laying out of a design throughout the Middle Ages. See the illustration accompanying GILDING.

USE

Use refers to a LITURGY practiced in a particular geographic region or by a particular group of people. The rites of the Christian liturgy developed along regional lines beginning in the EARLY CHRISTIAN period (producing, for example, Roman, Ambrosian, Gallican, and Mozarabic rites), although the Roman rite largely came to be regarded as the standard in the West. The texts of the MASS and the DIVINE OFFICE and their ordering throughout the year varied in accordance with these rites, with celebrations relating to local saints being particularly variable. The inclusion of local saints in CALENDARS and LITANIES can provide useful clues as to use. During the later Middle Ages, some uses were codified by cathedrals or major religious orders (such as the Sarum rite of Salisbury and the Paris rite) and consequently spread beyond their region of origin. In the sixteenth century, as part of the general spirit of Catholic reform, the Council of Trent (1545–63) abolished uses that were less than two hundred years old in favor of Roman use; in Protestant England, the Book of Common Prayer (1549) mandated the observation of one use throughout the realm.

In addition to a consideration of regional saints, use can be established by comparing certain elements of the text, such as the Psalm antiphons and the *capitula* for the hours of prime and none (see DIVINE OFFICE) to examples of known uses, but more reliable systems for identifying lesser-known uses continue to be explored.

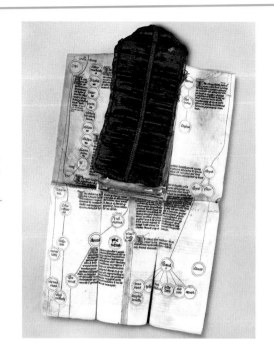

VADE MECUM
Notebook with a velvet cover, designed to be worn on a belt. England(?), early 15th century. 15×6.3 cm (5⅞×2½ in.). BL, Add. Ms. 17358.

VADE MECUM	The phrase means "goes with me" in Latin and refers to a portable book (often suspended from a belt), frequently consisting of leaves folded in a concertina or fold-out format. Such books could be consulted easily by physicians, for example, and often contain CALENDARS, almanacs, and medical information. See also ASTRONOMICAL/ASTROLOGICAL TEXTS, COMPUTUS TEXTS, GIRDLE BOOK, and MEDICAL TEXTS.
VELLUM	See PARCHMENT.
VERE DIGNUM MONOGRAM	See MISSAL and SACRAMENTARY.
VERNACULAR	A vernacular language is a regional language, as distinct from an international literary language, such as Latin and Greek. Throughout the Middle Ages certain texts, notably those of a liturgical character, were generally in Latin (although biblical texts were gradually translated into the vernacular). The development of Western vernacular literacy began at least as early as the sixth century in Ireland and CELTIC Britain and spread to England in the following century. Spain and Frankia followed suit later. The growth of secular literacy beginning in the twelfth century stimulated an increased use of the vernacular in texts. See also BIBLE.

VERSO

The back of a FOLIO or leaf, abbreviated as *v* and sometimes denoted as *b*.

VOLVELLE

A revolving wheel or wheels of PARCHMENT or PAPER (often within a book or attached to a BOOKMARKER) that carries information of a computational, astronomical, or astrological character. See the illustration accompanying MEDICAL TEXTS.

WATERMARK

See PAPER.

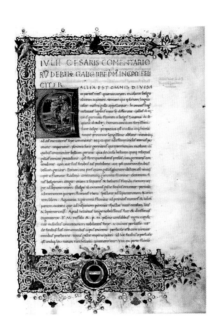
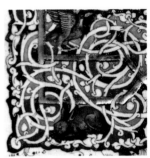

WHITE VINE-STEM
Initial *G* with *Caesar on Horseback*. Gaius Julius Caesar, *De bello gallico* and other works. Italy (Florence), c. 1460–70. 32.7 × 23 cm (12⅞ × 9¹⁄₁₆ in.). JPGM, Ms. Ludwig XIII 8 (83.MP.151), fol. 2 (full page and detail of border).

WHITE VINE-STEM

The Italian humanists (see HUMANISTIC) developed a characteristic white vine-stem BORDER (termed *bianchi girari*). The motif originated in fifteenth-century Florence and spread northward throughout Europe, accompanying humanistic or CLASSICAL TEXTS. White vine-stem borders were conscious emulations of what were thought to be ANTIQUE manuscripts but were in fact Italian manuscripts of the twelfth century. The white vine was generally left as blank parchment.

WORKSHOP

Also known by the French term *atelier*, a workshop is a studio in which a number of artists work together, generally under a MASTER, either on a regular or ad hoc basis. The term also refers to a group of artists who work together and is sometimes used in this sense to denote the secular equivalent of the monastic SCRIPTORIUM during the GOTHIC and RENAISSANCE periods (and during

ANTIQUITY as well). Artists working on the same project need not necessarily have belonged to a workshop, since they frequently lived in the same urban neighborhood and might join together for a single commission. In the context of attributing a work of art to a particular artist, the term "workshop product" is used when the art is in the style of a master, but is thought to have been executed by an assistant emulating that style. See also SCHOOL OF ILLUMINATION, SECULAR PRODUCTION, and STATIONER. See the illustration accompanying MASTER.

WRITTEN SPACE

See DIMENSIONS.

XYLOGRAPH

An image or text printed from a woodblock. During the later fifteenth and sixteenth centuries, xylographs occasionally appeared in manuscripts and were often hand-colored.

ZOO-ANTHROPOMORPHIC INITIAL

An INITIAL partly or wholly composed of conflated human and animal forms. Zoo-anthropomorphic EVANGELIST SYMBOLS, in which a human body is surmounted by the head of the symbolic animal, are occasionally found in INSULAR art and were particularly popular in Brittany. Zoo-anthropomorphic motifs also occur in other decorative contexts.

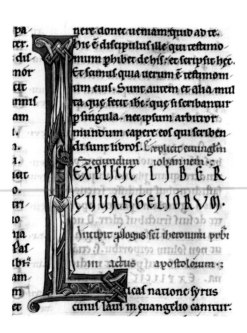

ZOO-ANTHROPOMORPHIC INITIAL
Initial *L* with *A Zoo-Anthropomorphic Symbol of Saint Luke*. New Testament. France (probably Pontigny), c. 1170. 43.5 × 31.5 cm (17⅛ × 12⅜ in.). JPGM, Ms. Ludwig I 4 (83.MA.53), fol. 95 (detail).

ZOOMORPHIC INITIAL

An INITIAL partly or wholly composed of animal forms. See the illustration accompanying PRE-CAROLINGIAN. Zoomorphic motifs occur in other decorative contexts as well.

Alexander, J. J. G. *Medieval Illuminators and Their Methods of Work.* New Haven and London, 1992.

Backhouse, J. M. *The Illuminated Manuscript.* London, 1979.

Baras, E., J. Irigoin, and J. Vezin. *La reliure médiévale: trois conférences d'initiation.* Paris, 1978, 1981.

Bischoff, Bernard. *Latin Palaeography.* Cambridge, 1990.

Boyle, L. *Medieval Latin Palaeography: A Bibliographical Introduction.* Toronto, 1984.

Brown, Michelle P. *A Guide to Western Historical Scripts from Antiquity to 1600.* London and Toronto, 1990.

De Hamel, Christopher. *A History of Illuminated Manuscripts.* Oxford, 1986.

————. *Scribes and Illuminators.* London, 1992.

Herbermann, C. G., et al., eds. *The Catholic Encyclopedia.* London, 1907–14.

Jackson, D. *The Story of Writing.* London, 1981.

Jakobi, Christine. *Buchmalerei: Ihre Terminologie in der Kunstgeschichte.* Berlin, 1991.

Lemaire, J. *Introduction à la codicologie.* Louvain-la-Neuve, 1989.

Loyn, H. R., ed. *The Middle Ages: A Concise Encyclopaedia.* London, 1989.

Muzerelle, D. *Vocabulaire codicologique.* Paris, 1985.

Needham, P. *Twelve Centuries of Bookbindings, 400–1600.* New York and London, 1979.

Pächt, O. *Book Illumination in the Middle Ages.* London, 1986.

Thompson, D. V. *Materials and Techniques of Medieval Painting.* New York, 1956.

Weijers, O., ed. *Vocabulaire du livre et de l'écriture au moyen âge.* Turnhout, 1989.

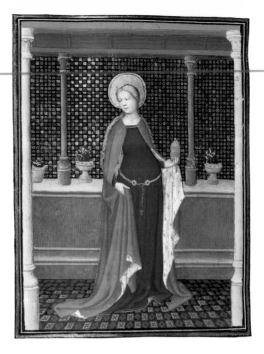

Workshop of the Boucicaut Master. *Saint Mary Magdalene*. Balfour Hours. France (Paris), c. 1415–20. 20.4 × 14.9 cm (8¹/₁₆ × 5⁷/₈ in.). JPGM, Ms. 22 (86.ML.571), fol. 137 (detail).

Sheila Schwartz, Editor

Kurt Hauser, Designer

Amy Armstrong, Production Coordinator

Charles Passela, Photographer

Eileen Delson, Production Artist

Typeset by Wilsted & Taylor, Oakland, California

Printed by Amilcare Pizzi, S.P.A.